Emotionally intelligent lawyers

•

How to navigate the psychological implications of becoming a lawyer

Esperanza Franco, Esq.

Illustrations by Azahara Clavero Fajardo
Cover design by Esperanza Franco and Paula Gorriz

ISBN: 978-84-09-50352-0

The ideas, exercises, and suggestions contained in this book are not intended as a substitute for therapy or consulting with a physician. The author is not responsible for any loss or damage allegedly arising from any information or suggestions provided in this book.

The author has tried her best to ensure any links to websites contained in this book are correct and accurate at the time of going to press. However, we cannot guarantee those links will remain live or that the content in them will still be relevant or appropriate. Moreover, many links needed to be formatted and shortened to fit within the margins of this book; which slightly deviates from the required internet citation rule under the Bluebook Legal Citation System Guide. The author has credited and cited other copyright holders when referring to any portion of their original works; but if there are any errors in or omissions, please notify the author at espy@esperanzaishope.com in order for her to rectify the errors for any reprints and future editions.

To my parents Rosa & Fernando, for raising me and supporting me in my American lawyer dream.

To 'Uncle Jim,' for always believing in me.

To my friends Danielle, Claire & Courtney, for lovingly reviewing the very first draft of this work.

To my partner, for 'sailing' the ups and downs of this book's process with me.

And to every student in this world, for daring to fight and navigate the academic journey.

Contents

*

Know Thyself.

— African Proverb (also Socrates later on)

INTRODUCTION

First, welcome to these pages. I appreciate your presence and attention to this important matter! Though this book is written by a lawyer, I'll be using non-legal, conversational language as if we were talking over a cup of tea or coffee (except for chapter 1, which is pretty academic-ish). It would be nice if we could interact as you read through, but since we can't, I'll leave my email at the end in case you feel like sharing any epiphanies or thoughts about the book with me. I hope these pages make you think, reflect, and feel seen. So, without further delay, let's turn to the following question(s):

Why are most lawyers so stressed and unhappy? Why does the legal profession currently hold one of the highest rates of depression and substance abuse of all occupations in the United States and in many other countries?

Some of the typical answers include:

Huge amounts of debt; lawyers are just mean and competitive people; really long hours at work; lots of money but no work-life balance; high pressure and deadlines; emotionally complex cases; they're always fighting against other lawyers or the government; really high expectations within the firm; the billable hour system…

Fair enough, Google (or my fav, *ChatGPT*). But here's something for us to consider:

If most factors are linked to the legal profession itself, why do we find similar levels of anxiety and depression in law students? *Why do law students suffer more stress than the general population if they haven't even become licensed lawyers yet? Are future lawyers some sort of type-A individuals who are already predisposed to psychological dysfunction; or* ***is this phenomenon in any way related to the educational training those future lawyers receive in law school?***

This book is dedicated to answering those questions; and it does so using an extensive body of empirical studies, experiential and multicultural knowledge, the sensitivity[1] to feel deeply, as well as a genuine desire to solve a structural problem from its root. As such,

- **Part I** answers the specific question of *why various forms of psychological distress appear within the first few months of law school attendance* (and, for the data-driven, it also covers

1 When I use the word sensitivity, I am referring to that of a Highly Sensitive Person ("HSP")—that is, an individual who tends to have an increased sensory processing sensitivity to physical, emotional, or social stimuli. If you're an HSP too, or just interested in learning more about this trait, I highly recommend "The Highly Sensitive Person," written by pioneer and psychologist Elaine Aron.

the most significant research done to date on law students' mental health).

- **Part II** dives into what it feels like to *live and think like a lawyer* in our world. From the 19th century-created identities and stereotypes, to the intricacies of the legal mind when it engages in excessive hypothetical negative thinking, competition, perfectionism, emotion*less* rationalism, empathic burnout, and so on.

- After that, **Part III** will take us to the emotional intelligence realms. We'll redefine obsolete lawyer identities and learn how to heal and manage our legal minds. (*Note*: once you make it to this phase, you'll need a notebook and a pen since it offers an interactive break from all the reading).

- Finally, **Part IV** is a call to action for law schools, institutions or any individual who has the power to safeguard the mental health of law students, advocate or implement positive changes in law schools.

That's it! It sounds simple but I promise it has taken years of research, setbacks, and work to be able to write it all. Apart from that agenda, my hope is that people who are, will, or have already suffered the rigors of law school will feel seen and validated by this book. This work also serves as a reminder that there are many of us out there who want to build a legal education system that integrates humanity and empathy.

Above all, I hope this book serves as a guide for law students, lawyers and law schools who are ready to start the healing process our profession desperately needs.

*

And may these writings serve as an ever-evolving manifesto

for the next generation of healthier,

emotionally intelligent lawyers.

And so it is.[2]

2 Always sending hugs to my witchy sisters out there ;)

Part i

•

Empirical data on the psychological impact of law school education

*

Since the 1970s, several researchers have documented that law school can be associated with high levels of anxiety and depression in law students. Interestingly, similar findings and conclusions repeat themselves today. While some have conjectured that law students share certain type-A attributes that make them prone to develop psychological disorders, empirical studies consistently show that part of the psychological distress students experience can be *directly traced* to law school's enrollment. In fact, according to longitudinal data, law students suffer more stress and anxiety than the general population, with various forms of psychological distress being acquired within the first few months of law school attendance.

If we acknowledge that many of those law students will hold crucial positions in legal and political life (or that stress is linked to a variety of severe illnesses), the responsibility to address a heavily-documented law student mental health crisis is a priority right now. More importantly, in order to solve a structural problem, we must first identify and analyze its origins and root causes. As such, that's what we're gonna do in the next four chapters:

Chapter 1 · Studies on Law Students' Mental Health: A Seventy-year Pattern

Ch. 2 · The "Socratic" Method in Law School Classrooms: Public Humiliation, *Reductio ad absurdum*, and the Student's Brain in *Fight-flight-freeze* mode

Disclaimer: Chapter 1 can become a little depressing or heavy since it contains what we consider to be theory or data-heavy texts about the issue. That said, I promise you two things: (1) it will help you integrate the teachings this book contains and equip you with a solid foundation for the problem we're trying to solve; and (2) it gets *muuuch* better after chapter 1, so please bear with me ;-)

1

Studies on Law Students' Mental Health:

A Seventy-year Pattern

The final and most persuasive reason for examining law school distress is that there is data indicating that the psychological distress experienced in law school simply foreshadows what many lawyers will experience after law school.

— Matthew M. Dammeyer & Narina Nunez, *Anxiety and Depression Among Law Students: Current Knowledge and Future Directions*, 23 L. & HUM. BEHAV. 55, 56 (1999).

Research on law students' mental health dates back to at least 1957, when a couple of clinical psychologists in the Psychiatry and Law Division at Yale University decided to study the effect of professional education on individuals, including those in legal education. One of the things they concluded was that legal training seemed to influence the student's personality and attitude formation. [3] Later in 1973, James Taylor surveyed first-, second-, and third-year law students from the University of Kansas Law School.[4]

Taylor also found that law school produced a sort of "déformation professionelle." By this, he meant that the high levels of stress law students were experiencing led them to adopt shared attributes, behaviors, values, and traits as ways of surviving and reducing anxiety (we'll dive into each of those in *Chapter 5 · The [19th Century] Lawyer Identity* and *Chapter 6 · The Legal Mind*). More specifically, Taylor argued that "the large and impersonal law school classes, the case study approach, the 'Socratic' method of teaching, [and] the harsh competition among students, are all claimed to create warping of personality and an undermining of ethical and social values."[5]

The same is true today, but let me show you this pattern more thoroughly (or in other words, please buckle up for the data-based journey I was talking about!).

---

3 Leonard D. Eron & Robert S Redmount, *The Effect of Legal Education on Attitudes*, 9 J. Legal Educ. 431, 431-443 (1957).

4 James B. Taylor, *Law School Stress and the "Déformation professionelle"*, 27 J. Legal Educ. 251, 251-267 (1975).

5 *Id.* at 251.

In 1986, Andy Benjamin and his colleagues conducted a longitudinal study[6] to assess any symptoms of psychological distress in Arizona law students *before enrolling, during, and after* completing law school. Because the study measured pre-law students, it also offered a more realistic insight into whether students' stress levels could have a causal connection with law school's enrollment. First, Benjamin found that before law school, pre-law students' symptoms did not differ from those of the general population. Moreover, the study found the following:

- **Students' distress scores were normal before entering law school** and those students were not necessarily predisposed to psychological disorders.
- However, once they enrolled in law school, those students' **symptoms of psychiatric distress significantly increased during their first year of law school,** as compared to those of the normal population.

Once they started law school, 17-40% of the surveyed students and alumni suffered from depression and 20-40% had other elevated distress symptoms. These symptoms included: obsessive compulsiveness, interpersonal sensitivity, anxiety, depression, hostility, phobic ideation, paranoid ideation, and psychoticism (social alienation

6 Andrew Benjamin, Alfred Haszniak, Bruce Sales & Stephen Shanfield, *The Role of Legal Education in Producing Psychological Distress Among Law Students*, 1986 AM. B. FOUND RES. J. 225, 236-47 (1986) (measuring, repeatedly and at different time intervals, 320 law students and alumni from the University of Arizona Law School). Instruments used in the study included the *Brief Symptom Inventory*, the *Beck Depression Inventory*, the *Multiple Affect Adjective Checklist* and the *Hassles Scale*.

and isolation). Upon graduation, these symptoms persisted and/or increased over the next two years of the young lawyers' careers.

In 1991, a nationwide study[7] showed that law students were using alcohol to cope with the high rates of stress. In this study, the Association of American Law Schools (AALS) surveyed 19 law schools and retrieved 3,388 individual responses from students. The survey showed that the increase and frequency of alcohol abuse among students *progressed* throughout law school. This pattern was later corroborated by the 2014 Survey of Law Student Wellbeing that we'll cover in a moment.

In 2000, another longitudinal study[8] showed that law students' levels of depression were similar to those of the general population before starting law school—which also argued against the theory that law students are just predisposed to develop psychological disorders. The study also showed that the surveyed law students showed significant changes in negative affect after beginning their classes, emphasizing the "similarity of [the students'] depression levels at the end of the first and third years to those of individuals who had undergone major life traumas."[9]

Likewise, a 2003 study[10] addressed pre-law students and compared law students to undergraduate students; again finding a significant decline in students' psychological well-being, physical

---

7 Association of American Law Schools Commission Report, *Report of the AALS Special Committee on Problems of Substance Abuse in the Law Schools*, 44 J. Leg. Educ. 35, 36-80 (1994).

8 Alan Reifman et al., *Depression and Affect Among Law Students During Law School: A Longitudinal Study*, 2 J. Emotional Abuse 93, 93–106 (2001) (the researchers studied a cohort of law students at the University of Michigan during the three years of their law school education).

9 *Id.* at 102.

10 Mary E. Pritchard et al., *What Predicts Adjustment Among Law Students? A Longitudinal Panel Study*, 143 J. Soc. Psychology 727, 727-45 (2003).

health and attitudes during their first year of law school. In 2004, behavioral health scholars published similar results,[11] noting that law students experienced significant **decreases in life satisfaction, wellbeing, and positive affect** during their first and third years of law school; and that while students began with higher levels of subjective well-being (SWB) than some undergrads, these levels had "plummeted" by the end of their first year in law school.

In 2007, another longitudinal study[12] showed that law students' psychological symptoms **significantly worsened after they enrolled in law school**. The authors also noted that being in law school, as well as the institutional culture itself, could be responsible for directly corroding law students' well-being, values, and motivation.

[mindful interruption]

Okay, let me pause for a second here. I know this can feel like a lot of data, so I'll add something about my law school story to somewhat compensate. To tell you the truth, I considered myself to be in those percentages. I suffered plenty while I was in law school and I can safely say that I saw the distress symptoms[13] researchers talked

11 Kennon M. Sheldon et al., *Does Legal Education Have Undermining Effects on Law Students? Evaluating Changes in Motivation, Values, and Well-being*, 22 BEHAV. SCI. & LAW 261, 261-86 (2004).

12 Kennon M. Sheldon & Lawrence S. Krieger., *Understanding the Negative Effects of Legal Education on Law Students: A Longitudinal Test of Self-determination Theory*, 33 PERS. & SOC. PSYCH. BULL. 883, 893-97 (2007).

13 Somatization, obsessive-compulsiveness, depression, anxiety, hostility, phobic ideation, paranoid ideation, psychoticism in the form of isolation and alienation…

about not only in myself, but in many of my law school friends and colleagues as well. As someone who has pursued three different law degrees and attended three different legal institutions, I have had the opportunity to observe, feel, and experience many of these things.

I was born and raised in the Canary Islands (Spain). I first went to law school in Madrid (ICADE)—though I had always dreamed of becoming an American litigator. I used to watch *Ally Mcbeal*... and when very little, I'd record myself speaking in my own invented version of English! Then, when I became a teenager, I spent a year in Arkansas to improve my English. In reality, though, that year served to spark my interest in social justice advocacy. I saw a lot of racism. I would tell my non-American friends what I was witnessing, and they would say: *En serio? Wow, I thought that didn't exist anymore!* I won't derail from the conversation here, but I'm sure you can imagine the type of things I saw and heard.

Anyway, even when I was studying in Madrid, my eyes were always set on the US (I just didn't have enough money to go to undergrad there and then do law school, so I patiently waited for my moment). I built my resume accordingly. Thus, once I graduated from ICADE, I got a traineeship as a foreign attorney at a law firm in Detroit and then interned at the Organization of American States in Washington D.C. Then I applied and was admitted to the University of Pennsylvania [now Carey] Law School, where I completed an LL.M. (Master of Laws) and got a partial scholarship. My parents asked for a loan on our house to help with my education. While I was there, I fiercely tried to transfer from the LL.M. to the J.D. program, but I didn't make the cut. Though ICADE was pretty competitive, Penn Law was the first time I truly interacted with the intensity and competitiveness of the U.S. law school system. As the LLM class president that year, I also tried to advocate for more compassion within the classroom, since many professors would cold-call on students whose English was not their first language, and therefore, sometimes needed the question to be repeated, for example. Likewise, my American colleagues in Student Government were also advocating for more empathy and racial awareness within the law school classroom.

Coming from a different legal system and culture allowed me to perceive things differently. I was able to watch the system *from the outside*, so to speak. Since my goal was to transfer to the J.D. program, I also became very close with the "1Ls," who were *always* studying at the library—just like me. This allowed me to witness the desperation, anxiety, and stress all these brilliant and highly-achieving individuals were going through.

When I found out I didn't get into the J.D. program (only two people transferred), my sense of worth plummeted momentarily, but I kept pushing for what I saw as my *American Lawyer Dream.* Since my parents could not support me for a year while I studied for the LSAT (note that as a non-English speaker who was not used to standardized tests, I was at a disadvantage and definitely needed at least that amount of time to prepare), I had two months to find programs that would give me some sort of advanced standing for being a foreign lawyer and therefore allow me to apply without an LSAT score.

That summer of 2014, I started my J.D. at the University of Arizona, James E. Rogers College of Law. In that moment, I switched from somewhat experiencing some pressure, to fully experiencing the pressure of a 1L (plus the added fact that I was an immigrant). As an immigrant law student in the US, I would need sponsorship from law firms. This meant I was already an undesirable candidate. It's much cheaper and less risky to hire an American citizen or a green card holder with worse grades. I won't get into the technicalities of sponsorship, the visa lottery, or other immigration-based considerations, the point was this: *if I wanted to get hired, I had to excel. Period. I could not afford not to stand out.*

The advantage I did have was that, thanks to Penn law, I knew what the stakes were from my very first day of class. I knew how incredibly competitive things would quickly get, especially at a non-top-14 law school in the US. And for me, my mantra was that not being the best also meant not being able to stay in the US and practice the career I had invested so much time and money in. This fact put an incredible amount of pressure on my psyche, but I wasn't the only person under pressure. There were mothers with kids, native Americans and African Americans in fully white-dominated classes, non-English speakers and first-generation students trying to navigate an unfamiliar system, or students with more than one hundred thousand dollars in debt. And while not everybody has experienced high levels of stress in law school, many have.

As classes progressed, I started seeing the same anxiety and depression patterns in Arizona law students that I had seen in Penn law students. That's when I decided to write my law review note on the psychological impact of law school education—which planted the real seed of this book.[14] In every single law school experience

14 I'll be forever grateful to a law school colleague named Zack, who brought me a physical copy of Benjamin's article on law student distress. Even though it wasn't a hot topic at the time (2016),

I had—from classes, study groups, or even "free time"—me and most of my colleagues struggled with some form of perfectionism, anxiety, depression, obsession with performance, extreme competition, or isolation. I was so puzzled. *Something is really wrong with this system*, I thought. Interestingly, in none of the law schools I attended did we ever talk about mental health, let alone the emotional intelligence required to practice law.[15] Nobody talked about whether they were medicating themselves (more about this later in *Chapter 3 · The Hunger Games*). Nobody talked about whether our personal lives were falling apart because of law school. We just acted like everything was *fine* because saying otherwise was seen as a clear sign of weakness. And if this just sounds like a personal experience, let's get back to the studies—we're almost done!

A 2009 study[16] of 140 students from the George Washington University Law School also found that more than half of the law students (53%) scored above a 16 on the CES-D scale, which is the **threshold for a clinically significant level of depression.** Furthermore, in 2014, the extensive Survey of Law Student Wellbeing[17]

I rolled with it anyways; and I never submitted the note for publication because the rebel in me did not agree with the fact that most journal articles are exclusively limited to the academic community (i.e., through a paid membership on HeinOnline, JSTOR, etc). I wanted and waited to birth a book that could be affordable and accessible to non-academics, as well.

15 With exceptions of course— among those, I was lucky to find Profs. Alicia Duñaiturria at ICADE, Shannon Browning and Gideon Parchomovsky at Penn Law, as well as Jane Bambauer and Toni Massaro at Arizona Law. They were all kindred souls who saw the importance of humanity in law school and legal practice.

16 Todd David Peterson et al., *Stemming the Tide of Law Student Depression: What Law Schools Need to Learn from the Science of Positive Psychology*, 9 YALE J. HEALTH POL'Y L. & ETHICS 357, 409, 411 (2009).

17 Jerome M. Organ, David B. Jaffe & Katherine M. Bender, *Suffering in Silence: The Survey of Law Student Wellbeing and the Reluctance of Law Students to Seek Help for Substance Abuse and Mental Health Concerns*, 66 J. LEGAL EDUC. 116, 145 (2016) [hereinafter *"2014 SLSWB Study"*].

(hereinafter "2014 SLSWB Study") corroborated an **alcohol-abuse** pattern among fifteen different law schools. Specifically, the authors emphasized:

> Alcohol use should be seen as a concern. Law students appear to be drinking more now than they were twenty years ago. Nearly one-quarter of respondents reported binge-drinking two or more times in the prior two weeks [before taking the survey] and one-quarter of respondents screened positive on the CAGE assessment, which suggests further screening for alcoholism is appropriate.[18]

More importantly, the 2014 SLSWB Study showed a **link between an obsession with top performance and the use of prescription drugs without a prescription**, such as Adderall (discussed in more depth in *Chapter 3 · The 1L Hunger Games*). Additionally, both the 2014 SLSWB Study and the Yale Law School's report on mental health[19] showed a pattern in law students' reluctance to seek help when facing mental health concerns or drug abuse problems (also discussed in *Chapter 4 · [Institutionalized] Stigmatization of Mental Health Struggles*).

---

18 *Id.* at 145. The study also shows that alcohol consumption among law students seems to be more prevalent than among graduate students. *Id.* at 127. This conclusion is in accordance with the Core Alcohol & Drug Survey from the 1990s and the Healthy Minds Survey, which has been administered annually since 2007 at hundreds of college campuses across the US. *Id.* at 127.

19 Jessie Agatstein et al., *Falling Through the Cracks: A Report on Mental Health at Yale Law School* (Dec. 2014).

Moreover, a smaller study surveyed 316 law students at two law schools,[20] finding that **one third of the students experienced significant psychological distress.**[21] That same research showcased that,

> [O]ver half of the participants scored above the 84th percentile for depression (57%) and overall psychological distress (55%). Nearly half (46%) scored above the 84th percentile for anxiety.[22]

A global law student mental health crisis

While most of the studies regarding law students' mental health have been conducted in the US, the literature in other countries report very similar narratives. For example, an **Australian** study that was able to fully survey 206 law students, showed that "[c]onsistent with existing scholarship in this regard, the law student participants in this study reported significantly higher levels of anxiety and depression than members of the general Australian population in the same age

---

20 Andrea Flynn et al., *Law School Stress: Moving from Narratives to Measurement*, 56 Washburn L.J. 259, 268 (2017) (the participants were from a law school ranked in the Top 100 and another one ranked in the Top 20). Measures used included Academic Achievement, Brief Symptom Inventory, Demographics, Law School Stressor Measure (LSSM) and Social Readjustment Rating Scale Revised (SRRS-R). *Id.* at 268-69.

21 *Id.* at 273.

22 Andrea Flynn, et al., *The Mental Health Status of Law Students: Implications for College Counselors*, 22 J. Coll. Counseling 1, 7 (2019) (emphasizing the results of the previous study and assessing the role of law school stress in students' psychological symptoms and suggesting ways college counselors could help specific law school populations).

range."[23] Similarly, a **German** study[24] showed that at least one third of the law student participants met the criteria for some form of depression, with about 17.7% reporting they had suicidal thoughts in the last two weeks before the survey. In the **UK**,[25] scholars have also emphasized the need for a curriculum that includes the development of resilience competencies and the management of subjective well-being.

A multi-layered and complex crisis

Moreover, if we take into account other factors, such as race, gender, or sexual orientation, we also find a significant amount of suffering in students. A recent study articulated the clear cognitive dissonance BIPOC (Black, Indigenous, and People of Color) law students experience "when they are confronted with an 'intellectual mismatch of the world's racial realities on the one hand and the racial silence-cum-neutrality of their legal education on the other hand."[26] The study also noted the unique challenges BIPOC law students faced during the past three years, including how COVID

23 Natalie Skead et al., *Stress, Anxiety and Depression in Law Students: How Student Behaviours Affect Student Wellbeing*, 40(2) Monash Univ. L. Rev. 546, 571, 572 (2014); *see generally*, Norm Kelk et al., *Courting the Blues: Attitudes Towards Depression in Australian Law Students and Lawyers, Report,* Brain & Mind Research Inst. (University of Sydney, Jan. 2009); Norm Kelk et al., *Distress and Depression Among Australian Law Students: Incidence, Attitudes and the Role of Universities*, 32 Sydney L. Rev. 113, 114-17 (2010).

24 Nadja Rabkow et al., *Facing the Truth – A report on the Mental Health Situation of German Law Students*, 7 Intl J.L. & Psychiatry 1, 2-3 (2020) (the study surveyed 306 German law students).

25 Caroline Strevens, *Law Student Wellbeing in the UK: A Call for Curriculum Intervention*, 11 J. Commonwealth & L. Legal Educ. 44, 45-56 (2016) (using the research done in Australian law students, and the similarity in legal educational systems, to advocate for the integration of principles of positive psychology and self-determination theory in legal curriculums).

26 Sarah J. Schendel, *Listen!: Amplifying the Experiences of Black Law School Graduates in 2020*, 100 Nebraska L. Rev. 73, 75-76 (2021) (citing the words of Professor of Law Shaun Ossei-Owusu).

disproportionately impacted communities of color, daily coverage of death and police brutality against black lives, and the pervasiveness of racist movements before and around the 2020 election. Words by Penn Law Professor Shaun Ossei-Owusu are illustrative here: "*For minority law students, learning the law can be intellectually violent.*"[27]

Likewise, a study[28]explored how sexism, homophobia, and racism produce microaggressions that damage the mental health of graduate and law students who identify as women, LGBTQIA+ and/or people of color, finding that heterosexual men reported significantly fewer types of microaggressions than all of the aforementioned groups. As for gender dynamics, a small study from the University of Chicago Law School[29] showed significant disparities between men and women in law school, with women experiencing negative gendered interactions in the classroom and reporting lower rates of satisfaction than men.

As the data suggests, legal education might prove alienating to individuals who do not fit into the white (cis) American male student stereotype from the nineteenth century (paradoxically, that student no longer even exists). And the *timing* and the historical context is indeed important here, because many law schools continue to use

---

27 Shaun Ossei-Owusu, *For Minority Law Students, Learning the Law Can Be Intellectually Violent*, ABA J. (Oct. 15, 2020, 11:23 AM), https://www.abajournal.com.

28 Kaitlin M. Boyle et al., *Microaggressions and Mental Health at the Intersections of Race, Gender, and Sexual Orientation in Graduate and Law School*, 15 J. Women Gender & Higher Educ. 157, 158-180 (2022) (this study analyzed a non-representative sample of 2,051 cisgender graduate students in a predominantly white university located in the southeastern region of the US).

29 Mallika Balachandran et al., *Speak Now: Results of a One-Year Study of Women's Experiences at the University of Chicago Law School*, 2019 Univ. Chi. L. Forum 647, 675-83 (2019); *see generally*, Lani Gunier, Becoming Gentlemen (Beacon Press 1997) (arguing, among others, that traditional legal education is alienating to women).

the same teaching methods that were used one hundred fifty years ago. When the modern American law school system—as we know it today—was consolidated in the 1870s, segregation was normal, lynching and killing black men was socially accepted (slavery had just been abolished a few years before), Chinese immigrants were expelled without justification, and women could not vote. That should tell us something about the need to update the *institutional software* a bit.

Now that we made it to the last paragraphs of this chapter (and take that as an accomplishment because this chapter is intense!), we have to ask: What's the latest update?[30] Where do we stand now?

The most recent (and comprehensive) study before this book headed out to the printer is the updated version of the 2014 SLSWB Study. The 2021 Survey for Law Student Wellbeing[31] (hereinafter "2021 SLSWB Study") is a huge undertaking[32] that reached 24,000 J.D. law students from 39 law schools and was able to retrieve full surveys from 5,400 law students. Apart from readdressing previous topics regarding law students' alcohol abuse, street drug use, prescription drug overuse, as well as mental health and help seeking

30 Unfortunately, COVID hasn't made things easier either. According to a study during the spring of 2020, 37% of law students experienced clinically significant symptoms of generalized anxiety disorder and 27% experienced clinically significant symptoms of major depressive disorders. *See* Soria Krista et al., *Law Students' Mental Health During the Covid-19 Pandemic*, UC Berkeley: Center for Studies in Higher Educ. 1-7 (2021), https://escholarship.org/uc/item/8t2668mk (the sample contained 644 law students at four public research universities).

31 David Jaffe et al., *It is Okay to Not Be Okay: The 2021 Survey of Law Student Well-Being*, 60 Univ. of Louisville L. Rev. 1, 2 (2022) [hereinafter *"2021 SLSWB Study"*].

32 I feel the need to say a special thanks to David Jaffe, one of the authors of both the 2014 and 2021 SLSWB studies, as well as Andy Benjamin (author of the most important longitudinal study conducted on this topic) because their work and dedication to this issue have been such a source of inspiration for me.

behaviors; the study also examined law students' experiences with trauma and concerns related to the bar exam. Here are some interesting results:

- The **use of stimulants without prescription** (such as *Adderall*) was still the most common shared drug with other law students, just as in the 2014 SLSWB Study. **Sedatives and anxiety medication** ranked as the second most frequently used. Among the students who indicated that they were using prescription drugs without a prescription, "a majority of those using sleeping medication, sedatives or stimulants all indicated that their recent use had increased compared to the twelve-month period prior to starting law school."[33]

- Moreover, **68.7%** of law students reported that they needed **help for emotional or mental health problems** in the last twelve months (this percentage increased, as compared to the 2014 SLSWB study). Specifically:[34]

    - While 32.7% of participants reported that they had been diagnosed with **depression** in their lifetime, 18% were diagnosed *after* they had started law school.
    - While 39.8% of law students reported a diagnosis of **anxiety** in their lifetime, 22.5% were diagnosed with it *after* they started law school.

---

33 *Id.* at 22.

34 *Id.* at 23-27 (the study also contains other categories covering eating disorders and non-suicidal self-harm).

- o When it came to **suicidal thoughts**, nearly 33% of law students had seriously thought about attempting suicide in their lifetime, with 11% thinking about it in the last twelve months before the survey, and 5% in the past thirty days.
- o Over 80 percent of the law students said[35] they had experienced some sort of **trauma**[36] in their lifetime, with one in five law students screening positive for post-traumatic stress disorder (PTSD).[37]

Imagine that one law student who is experiencing really high levels of anxiety or depression but who is simply too scared of saying anything out of fear it would mean the end of his career or status in law school. That student decides to "suck it up" and continues—just until his mental chatter gets way too loud. Remember the scene from the movie Paper Chase where the law student thinks about committing suicide during his first semester? Some may look at the numbers and say, '*well, it's not like it's the whole law school class - just some people.*' But the problem with mental health struggles is that they're invisible until something dramatic hits us. And most of the time we don't pay attention until something tangible—and bad—happens.

Take my less dramatic example. Right after the end of my 1L fall semester, I suddenly felt a desperate need to get a prescription

35 There are obvious limitations to self-reporting studies, but the body of research on law students' mental health is vast, diverse, and in many instances longitudinal.

36 The questions around trauma had fifteen categories, which included assault, sexual assault, serious illness or injury, emotional or physical abuse, accidents, natural disaster, etc. Those who expressed they had experienced one or more categories of trauma were given a PCL-5 to complete, which is a self-report instrument used in PTSD screening.

37 *Id.* at 43.

for Adderall. I was having racing thoughts: *'What if I mess up my GPA this second semester? How will I keep it up if we'll have an extra core subject? I need to be at 150%. I cannot make any mistakes.'* And so I made an appointment with a psychiatrist on campus, thinking that maybe they would prescribe me the stimulant to better concentrate, and therefore continue to *compete* for grades. I still remember telling the psychiatrist how I was having obsessive thoughts about my performance and how I needed to be perfect during my second semester. I remember saying, *I cannot afford to mess up or lose concentration.* And she listened quietly to all of that. And after I finished, she said something like:

> *You don't need Adderall. What you need is to calm the obsessive thoughts as well as reduce the high pressure and anxiety you're feeling.*

So there, and for the very first time in my life, I was given my first psychotropic prescription. This medication (called Sertraline), as she explained, was going to help me deal with my obsessive thinking or potential OCD.[38] I had never been diagnosed with OCD, anxiety or depression before (and I wasn't diagnosed at that session, either). Luckily, the psychiatrist explained that I did not have to take that medication for the rest of my life, but mainly for the time in which the very stressful event —the end of my 1L year— was taking place. In all honesty, I have never been a fan of medication but I was so desperate for help. So I did what I had to do in order to survive 'the

38 OCD is one of the psychological symptoms Andy Benjamin and colleagues found in law students upon law school enrollment. *See supra* note 6.

law school game.' The only thing I could do was to promise myself I would stop taking the medication at the end of my second semester and find more natural, alternative ways to deal with the problem (and thankfully, I kept my promise). *But no way José*... After the 1L horror ended, I knew there was something really off with the system. And while I had already "adapted" to the pressures of law school by that time (*aka* hyperproductivity became my *maladaptive* coping mechanism), I promised myself to understand why I—and so many others—had fallen into an extreme place of pain, desperation, and isolation. But ey, don't take my word for it—take the data.

A final summary

The body of empirical research done until today shows a pattern that looks like this:

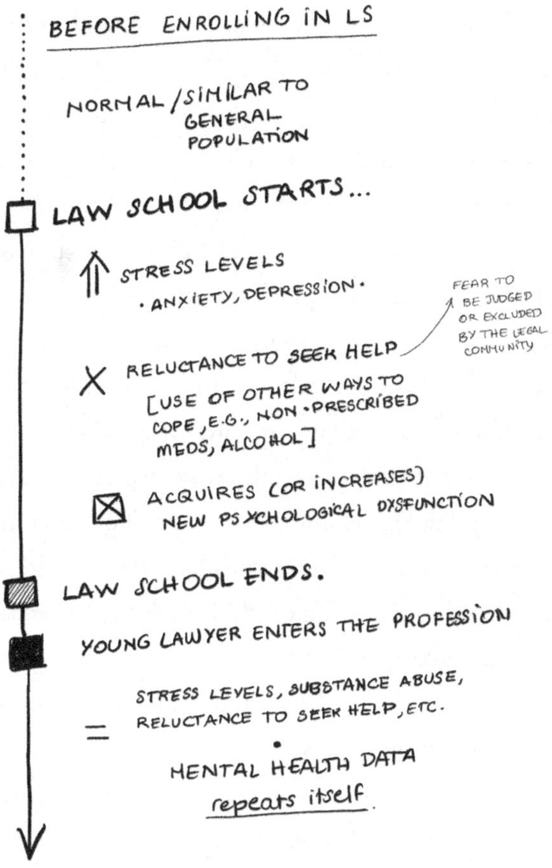

A somewhat chronological representation of the pattern we keep seeing in the studies on law student (and lawyer) mental health.

Or in other words, before entering law school, law students have a psychological profile similar to the normal population. Once enrolled, law students' levels of stress dramatically increase, with plenty of them leaving school with a psychological dysfunction. During law school, law students deny their stress levels and in turn use less effective ways to cope, such as with alcohol or non-prescribed medication. And even if they're struggling, they are reluctant to seek help, out of fear they will be judged or excluded by the legal community. *Et voilà*, law school is over and those same students enter a profession that will require emotional intelligence in order to navigate and thrive with the stressors in it! I guess the articles on '*Lawyers are more prone to depression*' are starting to make sense.

I often wonder: is it even fair that many law students are entering an educational system that can potentially destroy their mental health? Or is such institutional education worth upwards of two hundred thousand dollars (I'll write out the full number just in case: $200,000)? How is it possible to go to law school and leave with a new—or increased—psychological dysfunction? Respectfully, what type of contractual bargain is that?

We don't need more studies telling us that law school worsens law students' mental health. We know that. We need to come up with well-thought solutions. We need to start trying, implementing, and moving towards change. We need to revise (and somewhat eliminate) detrimental teaching techniques, once and for all. We need to invest in positive interventions. And no, offering a couple of mindfulness classes and free counseling on the law school's website isn't going to cut it. This problem is structural.

Sí, I get very passionate about it because I continue to see many law students struggle, and I don't want to keep seeing that. I also don't mean to say that law school damages everyone; but it damages enough people—at a significant enough rate—to warrant some sort of intervention. More importantly, access to the incredible body of data we have on law students' mental health provides *notice* to law schools. And while law schools don't damage their law students on purpose, they are responsible for providing a supportive education, or at least not one that causes major psychological damage. Don't you think?

With all that said, let us continue digging. The next issue for us to analyze is:

What *exactly happens inside* of law school?

In the next chapter, we are going to deconstruct the pedagogical techniques used in legal education[39] as well as the foundational pillars upon which the majority of law schools base their curriculums and teaching methodologies. Get ready for the dismantling!

---

39 Please note that this book is focused on American legal education, but many of the concepts also apply to other countries' legal educational systems.

2

The "Socratic" Method in Law School:

public humiliation, *reductio ad absurdum* and the student's brain in *fight-flight-freeze* mode

Closely related to the unrelenting pressure is the perceived humiliation of 'getting it wrong' in front of a large classroom brimming with one's peers. This method is utilized even early on in the first year, when students cannot reasonably be expected to have mastered the cognitive dexterity necessary to engage in the rigors of Socratic banter.

— Lauren Carasik, *Renaissance or Retrenchment: Legal Education at a Crossroads*, 44 IND. L. REV. 735, 749 (2011).

Columbus Langdell, Dean of Harvard Law School in the late nineteenth century, implemented the "Socratic" method in the law school classroom. He believed that "it was necessary that 'the student judge all material for himself, scrutinize instances closely, and accept no other man's judgment until he had judged its logic for himself'. . ."[40] In other words, according to Langdell, law students should not have the opportunity to *first* discuss complex cases with their experienced professors (and therefore learn from them). Rather, students are meant to absorb these complex pieces of information on their own and then, be *tested*—publicly—on those pieces of information. This chapter will analyze the following points:

- The Socratic method, as created and developed by the Greeks and its differences from the *version that is applied in law school.*
- The law student's brain when cold-called.
- Racial disparities, gender dynamics and trauma in the classroom.
- Consequences impacting engagement & participation.

The (Real) Socratic Method

It is necessary that we first understand how the Socratic method was designed and developed; and that we do so from the perspective of its very own creator, Socrates; and not as implemented[41] in

40 Alan A. Stone, *Legal Education on the Couch*, 85 Harvard L. Rev 392, 406 (1971).

41 "American legal education went badly wrong seventy years ago when it was seduced by a brilliant neurotic. I refer to the well-known founder of the so-called case system, Christopher Columbus Langdell. I call him a neurotic advisely. He was a cloistered, bookish man, and bookish,

law schools by Columbus Langdell. There is a significant difference between the two.

The Socratic method, also called *Elenchus*, is a teaching method that dates back to Ancient Greece.[42] Initially developed by Socrates, this method was based on the premise that, through an argumentative dialogue between individuals, one can deeply examine an issue, as well as any underlying beliefs and presuppositions.

As a form of *cooperative dialogue between equals*, this method was based on asking questions to think critically and eliminate the hypotheses that were contradictory or impractical. The process of elimination was commonly referred to as *reductio ad absurdum*, which means "argument to absurdity" in Latin and it seeks to rebut a scenario by showing it is absurd or impractical.

That process, however, would take place within a cooperative dialogue, and not as an adversarial and intimidating exercise. Per se, the purpose of Socratic discussions was not for the individual or the group to "win an argument," but to deeply examine an issue. The goal was for all of the individuals in the circle (or classroom) to gain a deeper understanding and consequently arrive at an answer.

---

too, in a narrow sense." Jerome Frank, *A Plea For Lawyer-Schools*, 56 YALE L. J. 1303, 1303 (1947). The author in this article further explained the philosophy that shaped every single educational program in law schools: "if it be granted that law is to be taught as a science and in the scientific spirit, previous experience in practice becomes as unnecessary as is continuance in practice after teaching beings. . . [a]s a consequence, . . . most teachers in those schools either had little or no experience in active legal practice or, more important, if they had, yet when they withdrew from practice to teaching, they succumbed to an atmosphere in which the memories of practice became shadowy and unreal. The Langdell spirit choked legal education. It compelled the experienced practitioner, turned teacher, to belittle his experience at the bar. It forced him to place primary emphasis on the library, to regard a collection of books as the heart of law school. . ." *Id.* at 1304.

42 *See generally*, Aristotle's *Prior Analytics* on Deductive Reasoning *and* Plato's Apology of Socrates.

An illustration of a Socratic discussion in Ancient Greece

Reductio ad absurdum, as applied in the law school classroom: perceived & public humiliation

The problem arises when the Socratic method is used in a hostile way; or when an added component—such as cold calling—shifts the power dynamic; thereby turning a healthy, intellectual discussion into a grilling test. Unfortunately, this new dynamic is what one finds in most law school classrooms, and why cold calling is so famously pictured as a terrorizing experience law students must go through.

In the famous 1973 movie *The Paper Chase*, Mr. Kingsfield, the Contracts Law Professor at Harvard Law School, starts applying the Socratic method and looks at a map with all of his first-year law students' names and faces. It is the first day of class. He then cold calls a student and starts questioning him about a case. Mr.

Kingsfield then continues to grill his victim on the case details and ends up humiliating that student in front of the class. Interestingly, this performance takes place in a typical (rounded) law school classroom, where almost everybody gets to watch the "show."[43]

Not so different from this 50-year-old movie, when a law student is cold-called in real life, that student is expected to be prepared to answer any question the professor asks about the case(s) assigned. Although the professor has not dissected and explained the case(s) in advance, law students are still expected to reason and reply to the questions posed as if they are experts—all in front of an audience, that is, in front of all of their law school classmates. Generally, the professor starts by asking the law student elucidative questions until that student takes a wrong or indefensible position, in which case, the professor starts attacking that position.[44] In some cases, the professor starts by asking very specific (and extrinsic) details of the case, even though those have no relevance when it comes to the issue, rule, or application in the case. This is how *reductio ad absurdum* takes form in the law school classroom. Here's a comparative chart of the differences from the real Socratic form:

43 If you haven't seen the movie, I recommend you google it or watch the scene on Youtube to get a better idea!

44 Apart from the stories that most law students talk about, I experienced this at both Penn Law and Arizona Law, though the latter was a bit less aggressive in their cold calling.

"Socratic" method as applied in law school	**Socratic method per se**
• *Power dynamics:* Professor represents the only authority.	• *Power dynamics:* Professor is not "the sage on the stage." Participants are equals having an intellectual conversation or examination of an issue.
• *Initiation of the discussion:* Prof. cold-calls on students, which means students have to passively wait to be cold-called. They do not initiate (unless the Prof. "allows" for participation rather than cold calling).	• *Initiation:* Professor starts guiding the conversation by posing thought-provoking questions and the back-and-forth discussion starts taking shape.
• *Progress:* it turns into a one-sided conversation where the professor always asks the questions and retains "power" in the dynamic. Other students passively witness their classmates' cold calls.	• *Progress:* the conversation naturally progresses as students actively engage by asking questions, analyzing and refuting presumptions in a collaborative way.

"Socratic" method as applied in law school	**Socratic method per se**
• *Substance of the discussion:* many questions focus on *details*, including extraneous ones that are irrelevant to the legal analysis. As such, many questions tend to have either a right or wrong answer since they're directed at testing the "details" of the case.	• *Substance of the discussion:* Focuses on the analytical question at hand. Questions are open-ended; there's no predetermined goal but merely the deep study of the issue.
• As a consequence, students obsess about this "testing of details" and try to memorize every single detail of the assigned cases in order to "survive" the cold-calling (public) moment; instead of critically thinking about the core analytical issues of the assigned cases.	• Because there's no "testing" or threat of "public humiliation," the students focus on seeking answers critically and creatively, not on performing in front of the audience.

"Socratic" method as applied in law school	Socratic method per se
• *Value of the discussion:* tends to move towards the "correct" answer to the Professor's questions, especially because of the established power dynamic. The student's focus is therefore on "getting in right" while the others watch their public performance.	• *Value* is only centered in the analysis or deep examination of the issue. The students' focus is on refuting, contributing and helping the group get to the truth or the answer to the difficult question.
• In many instances, the Professor becomes the "opponent," strictly using *reductio ad absurdum* to discredit the student's analysis in public.	• The Professor also acts as a "mind" in the dialogue, kindly listening to the person explain, or challenging the student's position with a sense of curiosity and camaraderie, rather than superiority, aggressiveness, and hostility.

As one law student said:

> And that's the thing. I feel like sometimes we are so scared of being cold-called that we focus more on the details of the cases we're reading instead of the actual, like, the actual core of what we're being taught through the case.[45]

While Greeks effectively used the Socratic method to develop mathematical and philosophical reasoning, we must ask: what happens when this method is used in a public, competitive, and intimidating setting like a first-year law school classroom? What happens when that classroom turns into a public show?

Here's the thing. We don't need to get rid of the Socratic Method or the *reductio ad absurdum*. We're lawyers. We think, argue, and analyze. But what we must *not* do is misapply an argumentative method in a way that creates a hostile and intimidating environment for students who are in the process of learning the law. We should apply it in the way it was intended: as a cooperative, collaborative, productive discussion. There's a huge difference between using this method to create dialogue in a safe, controlled environment *versus* using it to test law students about a complex case, for the first time, and in front of[46] their classmates (who are also their direct competitors, by the way):

45 Kathryne M. Young, *Understanding the Social and Cognitive Process in Law School that Creates Unhealthy Lawyers*, 89 FORDHAM L. REV. 2575, 2590 (2021) (quoting from an interview with a student).

46 Also, remember that most law school classrooms are laid out in a "circle" where everybody sees you. These classrooms recall the constant surveillance of Jeremy Bentham's concept of the panopticon, with a central observation point placed within a circle of prison cells. Maybe I'm being too dramatic about this, but if you've sat in a traditional law school classroom, you know exactly what I mean.

> In the [Socratic method], students are singled out and questioned intensely [...] in front of the class. The professor-student power difference, being singled out, and humiliation many feel, make this a particularly clear example of potential *abuse*.[47]

Let's quickly look at some data. A Pilot Program conducted at Stanford and Yale law schools (called *Anxiety Psychoeducation for Law Students*) began with an exercise to replicate the experience of being cold-called in law students. Specifically, the participants would hypothetically get cold-called; and during that cold call, they would start having difficulty locating the exact details of the case while the whole class was staring at them. Then the participants were asked to write down three automatic thoughts or emotions they felt during that hypothetical cold call. Some of the responses[48] were as follows:

- *I feel inadequate.*
- *I feel shame, embarrassment.*
- *I feel inferior to everyone.*
- *I felt exposed.*
- *I feel stressed—like I'm in a hole I can't climb out of.*
- *I feel disappointed in myself.*
- *I feel angry at myself/full of self-loathing.*
- *I feel stupid.*
- *Everyone thinks I'm stupid.*

---

47 Reifman et al., *supra* note 8, at 94 (emphasis added).

48 Ian Ayres et al., *Anxiety Psychoeducation for Law Students: A Pilot Program*, 67 J. Legal Educ. 118, 125-26 (2017) [hereinafter "*Anxiety Psychoeducation*"]

Then the participants were asked to write down how they would feel on the next day, after having been cold-called in class. Some of the answers[49] included:

- *I want to avoid everyone.*
- *I play it over obsessively in my mind.*
- *I think about all the things I should have said.*
- *I go over the case in my head so much it's not healthy.*
- *I'm mediocre.*
- *I'm less likely to raise my hand or participate next time.*

We know one thing for sure. The way many law schools have been applying—and continue to apply—the "Socratic method" does not benefit students. It directly creates distress in them. What more evidence do we need to implement change? How many more painful experiences do new law students need to have? While probing questions are meant to help a person think more deeply about an issue, there's a difference between safe and unsafe environments, especially when it comes to our nervous systems. It is different to be asked probing questions in a healthy environment where mistakes are <u>not</u> exposed or showcased, as compared to a hostile environment where everyone is looking at you, waiting for you to fail or make a mistake (because remember, law school is *that* competitive). Here's a student's description of exactly what I mean:

> I noticed myself, like, almost excited when people get things wrong, which is not…actually a normal thing. I would

49 *Id.* at 126.

> never, I would never, want people to get things wrong. But it means, like, if you're getting things wrong and I can get it right, it means I can be above the curve.[50]

And of course, further exacerbating the misapplication of the Socratic method is the grading curve and intrinsic competition of law school. Cold calling not only creates distress in law students; it also fosters an "attack" methodology within the legal field: *Let's see if you're truly that smart in front of everybody. Let's see if you don't make any mistakes, huh!* In fact, Bernard L. Diamond saw this phenomenon as a long-term problem in the student who now felt inclined to imitate this "attack" methodology and adopted a style of aggressive and sarcastic interrogation with his own clients; therefore creating in them the same feelings of harassment and anxiety that he himself experienced in law school.[51] Apart from the humiliation and hostility, does it even make sense to learn the complexities of the law in a hostile and intimidating environment from a psychological and pedagogical point of view?

The law student's brain in *fight-flight-freeze* mode

While law school's emphasis on a combat-dialogue in class is somewhat well-intended (it relates to '*thinking like a lawyer*' in an

50 Young, *supra* note 45, at 2586 (quoting from a student's interview).

51 *See* Stephen Gillers, *Looking at Law School IN* PSYCHOLOGICAL PROBLEMS OF LAW STUDENTS, 23 (Plume, 1997).

adversarial system), we still need to address how cold calling specifically affects the law student's mental health.

For starters, our brains cannot safely learn if we're in fight-flight-freeze mode. When we encounter a situation that creates anxiety, fear or stress, such as being cold-called in front of a class filled with people, our amygdala gets activated. Our amygdala[52] is like our alarm center and it also serves a primary role in the processing of our memories, decision making, and emotional responses. This means that when the amygdala "rings the alarm," it also mobilizes the resources in our body to respond to what it considers to be a threat. In order to do that, it has to decrease activation in our prefrontal cortex—the center for executive function in our brains—which in turn impairs our rational thinking and decision making. This process is called the "amygdala hijack"—a term coined by Daniel Goleman.

When the amygdala "hijacks" us, it puts us in what's called fight-flight-freeze mode, which is the body's automatic, built-in system to protect us from any threats or danger. If our brains detect a threat or a *perceived* threat (e.g., being humiliated in front of my peers, not knowing all the answers during the cold call, a loud noise, our boss criticizing our work product in front of our peers, being followed on the street, etc), our amygdala automatically activates an automatic response. This automatic response then turns into a physiological reaction that prepares our bodies to either fight, flee or freeze. When this happens, our bodies release stress hormones, including cortisol and epinephrine (also known as adrenaline). Have you ever gone blank when a professor asked you something, even if you studied

---

52 Technically, we have two amygdalae (each located close to the hippocampus), but I'll refer to it in the singular form throughout this book for simplicity purposes.

that case for hours? (*freeze*) Have you ever felt this desperate need to suddenly leave a place because you didn't feel comfortable there? (*flight*) Have you ever yelled at your partner or colleague because you automatically felt attacked, judged or criticized by something they said? (*fight*). There are many examples, but the following one is especially illustrative for us:

> [The] 'most negative part of law school' was . . . how much cold calls will stress me out a little bit after class. Just like messing up a question. And then thinking about what your answer should have been. But you blanked in that moment. Just like beating myself up.[53]

When our amygdala is activated, we may feel anxiety, anger, or fear, because our bodies are trying to respond to what they consider to be a threat. This physiological reaction happens automatically, whether we're conscious of it or not. Therefore, every time there exists a real possibility of getting cold-called (and/or humiliated in front of peers), a law student's amygdala will likely be activated—generating stress hormones and potentially putting the student in a fight-flight-freeze mode.

Imagine yourself (again) or a friend, as a first-year law student…

As you're fighting to keep up with the incredible amounts of reading, within the limited amount of hours in a day; as you're trying to understand cases from the 19th century; or as you're learning new

53 Young, *supra* note 45, at 2591 (quoting from a student's interview).

words that you've never heard before...you suddenly realize that you will be tested on all that reading material—which you may or may not have been able to finish before class—and in public, that is, in front of your classmates (whom you're are also competing against).

And you know. You know it's not enough to get a big picture of the cases you're reading... no. You must remember all the small, irrelevant details of the case, because unfortunately there are some professors who love to pick on those. And you don't want to look stupid. You don't want to look unprepared or unintelligent in front of your peers... because who does? Then to that anxiety and fear you're feeling, add to the ambiance the feelings from all of the other similarly stressed, nervous, and competitive law students in your class. That's the vibe, every day. Because every day, you continue to go to class and endure all the potential, or real, cold calling moments. And every day, you know that you cannot fall back in your readings because there is a curve. I mean, you know. You cannot get sick. Because if you do, you will fall behind on your reading assignments—and God forbid you get cold-called on something you have not read! Imagine the ridicule...

Imagine all of that, and voilà,
you have the [unbearable] life of a first-year law student.

Furthermore, for a law student, it's not just about the anxiety and anticipation of being cold-called; it's also about what it means to get it wrong in front of a class full of peers. Think of study groups, for example. I mean, there are some law schools where you need to submit an application to be part of a study group![54] Imagine then, the pressure to perform during a cold call.

Make no mistake. Cold calling cannot rest on the Socratic Method *per se* because that method involved a *shared dialogue between equals*—between intellectuals. Cold calling is not a conversation. It's a <u>test</u>. And many law professors cold call(ed) law students in order to test them (in public), not to converse with them in a friendly, collaborative way. And apart from administering a high dose of comparisonitis and imposter syndrome, cold calling can also create deep feelings of unworthiness:

> *I am terrible at this. I will never be a good lawyer. They'll always think I'm stupid. There's no way back now—I fuck*d up, in front of everyone. I guess I'm not as smart as everybody else. Nobody is gonna want me in their study group. I'm useless.*[55]

So one has to wonder, if cold calling has proven detrimental for the law student's mental health, why does it continue to be legitimized? We have more difficulty absorbing complex information when our amygdala 'rings the alarm' because the activation in our prefrontal cortex will decrease as a result; and so will our ability to rationally think and make decisions. Thus, how does cold calling continue to serve a pedagogical purpose? We now know that we learn better in healthy and supportive environments, so why do we keep injecting fear and intimidation to teach?

54 One of my best friends goes to a top 7 law school and narrated this anecdote of the study group's selection process to me.

55 I draw these mental narratives from my own experience, conversations with my students, as well as friends and fellow classmates who have actually endured a "bad" cold call in law school.

Furthermore, we need to take into account the aftermath of it all. This is what I mean: if these stressful, cold calling scenarios take place *every day*, what happens on a physiological level when the student's amygdala is *repeatedly* being activated in the classroom? What happens when, as we attempt to learn, our alarm system is constantly mobilizing our attention, as well as our emotional, and physiological resources to a perceived threat?

Well, we know one thing that will happen for sure: we'll have a group of pretty stressed and exhausted law students (which is also what the data tells us). Under this logic, does teaching using fear-based methods make sense? If cold calling is conducive to unsafe, stress-induced classroom environments where students are forced to experience unnecessary levels of distress, why do we keep using it?

Racial disparities, gender dynamics, and trauma in the classroom

Law school's version of the Socratic method can further alienate minorities.[56] Take, for example, an African American law student who is in his constitutional law class, reading an old (or not so old) case that deals with racial discrimination. Picture that student having to witness, in a law school class (that is, the cold-calling setting), another African American law student being grilled about the details of the case. Or better yet, another white student actively dismissing

56 I want to make something clear. I add this information because it's a reality that needs to be exposed, not because I self-proclaim myself an expert in it. I can only speak about my experience as an immigrant. Anything else I leave to the real experts, that is, those who have experienced it generationally or in their own skin (aka the *white savior complex* is getting really old and one cannot claim experiences that are not theirs).

the cruelty and discrimination the system has perpetuated over centuries. How does that student feel inside? What if he gets cold-called? What if the professor starts using *reductio ad absurdum* on how the discrimination *was* legitimate?

The issue here is not only whether the professor has enough empathy or humanity to address race in class—if only. It's about the possibility of retraumatizing a group of students who are implicitly expected to disassociate from their bodies[57] and behave as "emotionless rocks" in a cold-calling setting when their very humanity seems up for debate. How damaging is this experience for them? Do you think that student would feel safe in class—let alone voluntarily participate in the heated debate? Or do you think he might be suffering in silence, inside, waiting for the class to end? His body wanting to fight or flee?

Professor's Young 2021 study[58] can be illustrative when it comes to explaining harmful social processes inside of law school, especially in terms of race and gender disparities. Law school tends to be a predominantly white environment—with mostly white (cis) males dominating classroom discussions. In the study, Prof. Young describes how cold calls disproportionately affected women of color. Per the study, women of color felt as if they needed to know every single detail of a case and be one-hundred percent prepared to respond to any question; otherwise, they did not feel "ready." In contrast, white men did not express a similar struggle. Moreover, in smaller settings, such as Zoom discussion groups, most women felt that white males continued to dominate the conversation, often dismissing any woman's opinion.

57 Which are probably producing cortisol due to the amygdala's activation.

58 Young, *supra* note 45, at 2591-94.

Similar struggles can be seen in BIPOC law students, non-English speaking immigrant students, first-generation students, LGBTQIA+ students, or trauma[59] survivors when it comes to cold calling. As a whole, it is not rare to see law students skipping class in order to avoid the performative and mental anguish of cold calling.

A fear-based teaching system does not encourage participation

Follow-up question: does the cold calling ("Socratic method") hinder participation? Common sense will probably tell us that fear in a classroom will tend to discourage engagement and participation to some extent. Let's take a quick look at a small study done by Jeffrey Perrin et al.[60] This study surveyed a group of law students and found that the fear of peer judgment was a demotivating factor in the participants' learning experiences. Due to this fear, students were hesitant to participate in the classroom discussion, whether by expressing their opinions, or *even by just asking questions.*

The study also emphasized that most law students are scared of feeling unintelligent or irrelevant during class, which in turn resulted in participation withdrawal.[61] Many law students also reported logging out of the Zoom room to avoid getting cold-called. I mean,

---

59 If the law student already carries previous trauma—and, as we saw in the 2021 SLSWB Study, many law students do carry it before coming to law school— a highly stressful environment is only going to worsen that student's sense of self and mental health.

60 Jeffrey Perrin, et. al, *Do Learners Fear More than Fear Itself: The Role of Fear in Law Students Educational Experiences*, 2 J. Education & Training Studies 67, 67-75 (2014).

61 This pattern is also connected to the 'feeling worthy of being chosen by a study group' dilemma I mentioned earlier. For the sake of survival, joining a study group (if the student decides to join one), can be important to prepare for exams.

one can only imagine adding the *reductio ad absurdum* to the mix of intensive questioning during a cold call. Because the thing is, if you ask a clarifying question or try to make a comment, how do you know you won't be put on the "cold-calling spot"? One friend described it as if the punishment for wanting to understand things better was humiliation.

In most of my 1L classes, not participating or avoiding eye contact with the Professor was my personal reaction. I took notes and stayed quiet; but in reality, there were many times I had things to say or add to the 'discussion', but it felt too risky to be put on the "humiliation" spot. So I kept silent to keep myself safe, just in case. I tried to protect myself from the potential distress I could experience if I suddenly messed up an answer. I just wanted to make it through the day, feeling emotionally 'okay'.

As with fixed mindsets,[62] cold calling can turn into an all-or-nothing situation devoid of any room for growth. You either nailed the cold call or you didn't—at least in the student's mind, which is why it's so common to hear them say how they go over every detail of a cold call in their head and beat themselves up afterwards about all of the things they could and should have said. Designed as a combat dialogue and as a public test—rather than a safe discussion—cold calling is inevitably tainted by a harsh, overly perfectionistic mentality.

From a pedagogical perspective, a teaching method that reinforces fear, humiliation, and feelings of unworthiness is counterintuitive.

---

62 A fixed mindset is a belief that intelligence or talent are fixed traits that cannot be changed or developed. As such, individuals with a fixed mindset believe that their success or failure are largely determined by those innate abilities and qualities; therefore, leaving no room for improvement or growth. This term is also discussed in depth in Chapter 5.

In fact, one cannot expect first-year law students to master a highly complex case that has not been explained in advance to them by their educators, let alone expect them to publicly demonstrate such 'mastery' in front of an audience. As the study described it,

> Humiliation, lack of control, and isolation were amongst the various emotional themes identified by the researchers. The stress and anxiety levels of students at the end of their first and third years was similar to those individuals going through a major life trauma . . .[63]

We can do better. We can implement more positive methods to teach law students.[64] We can foster more understanding, empathic, and sensitive debates. The Socratic method was originally designed as a mechanism to foster creative and critical thinking, not as a testing tool to intimidate students. And while cold calling might make the job of some professors easier, it certainly creates emotional detriment in law students and it hinders healthy participation—and that in itself should be enough to question its use and legitimacy. In our current (modern) era, do we really want to continue to teach the law through fear and humiliation?

63 *Perrin, supra* note 60, at 68.

64 We discuss how in Parts III and IV.

3

The 1L Hunger Games:

The Curve as a Filter for Law Firms, Pathological Competition, and the Shift in the Student's Sense of Worth

The [law] student is stripped naked, so to speak, so that he may be remade a lawyer. The underlying dynamic, I suspect, parallels a highly structured, controlling, emotionally intense initiatory rite used by the church or the military in the indoctrination of their neophytes.

— J. C. Halpern, *On the Politics and Pathology of Legal Education*, 32 J. LEGAL EDUC. 383, 388-89 (1982).

In this chapter, we'll cover the following points:

- The law school grading curve.
- The curve as a filter for law firms.
- Psychological implications: an obsession with performance and pathological competition on the curve, as well as a shift in the student's sense of worth.

The law school grading curve—*defined*

Law school grading (especially during 1L year) is generally done on a strict bell curve, often called the Gauss Curve. This means that the exact number of As, A-s, Bs, B+s, B-s, Cs and so on is already predetermined. Even if twenty students each turn in an exam that, objectively, meets the professor's expectation for an A, only a few of them will get that A. Here's a visual example of what a real life 1L curve tends to look like:

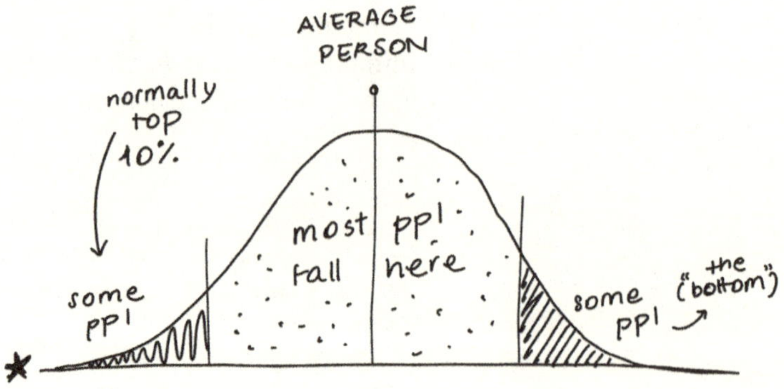

An approximate representation of the 1L curve in real life.

Though it depends on each law professor, only 10% or fewer of students in a given class will generally get that A under a Gauss Curve.[65] Likewise, another 15% or fewer will get an A-. The rest will get B+, Bs or lower—that is, the remaining 75% of the class. In other words, more than half of the people will fall in the middle of the curve, unable to reach the top. However, almost everybody will try to get to that top 10%.

To reiterate, mostly every student wants or *needs* to get to that top—especially in non-top-tier 14 law schools. First, making it to the top of the curve directly impacts access to job opportunities; that is, the student's later ability to pay off their loans and make a living. Many law students in the U.S. are graduating with at least two hundred thousand dollars in debt. Second, most law students are high-performing individuals who have worked extremely hard to make it to law school in the first place; therefore, they will likely try to reach that top as well.

This means we'll have a class where the majority of the students are competing against each other for grades. But, as explained, it is mathematically impossible that most of them will make it to that top 10 percent, regardless of how diligent and hard-working they are when studying and turning in their exams. What will happen is that the majority will fall in the middle of the curve. And this wouldn't be a problem if 1L grades did not matter so much, but they do matter—a lot. In fact, grades will directly translate into: class ranking, law review membership, and ultimately, the student's first job opportunities out of law school.

---

65 The distribution will depend on each professor but these are approximate percentages to explain this process.

Designed as a filter for law firms, grades end up operating like a "pedigree" measurement that will have a direct impact on a law student's access to her first job placement, and will therefore control the student's short-term future and ability to repay her debt in the mid- or long-term.

A filter for law firms

When I was a pre-law student doing research on how to succeed in law school, I came across an article where Erwin Chemerinsky noted: "the reality, we were told over and again, is that employers depend on [law] schools to sort students out through a grading system."[66]

So yes, 1L grades have historically served as a streamlining process for law firms. Through on-campus interviewing ("OCI"), employers rely on grades in order to recruit their summer associates. This process is frequently as follows: based on their rankings, law students bid for law firms, and law firms then select the students who have made the cut for an interview. The problem, however, is that for non-T-14 law schools (we're talking approximately 186 law schools, if we consider the 200 ABA-accredited law schools in the U.S.), law firms tend to establish a cut-out system, where only those at the top 25% or higher can even apply to be interviewed. This means that law students who did not make it to the top 25% (i.e., 75% of the class) simply cannot apply.

This system also means that a law student's opportunity to get to the first layer of recruiting will completely depend on their grade

---

66 Erwin Chemerinsky, *The Ideal Law School for the 21st Century*, 1 UC Irvine L. Rev. 1, 23 (2011).

ranking. The same happens with federal clerkships, where law review membership (which is also mostly determined by grades) tends to be a requirement for entry, as well. As such, a law student's 1L grades will mostly determine their initial career opportunities. This inevitably makes law school a very competitive environment *per se*, and law students interiorize very early on that they are, in fact, competing against their classmates.

Obsession with performance and pathological competition on the curve

I am not saying that law school needs to turn into flowers and sunshine. Competition creates development, innovation, and growth. In fact, a certain amount of academic stress is necessary for optimal performance. Otherwise, the student would not care at all—missing deadlines, assignments, and many of the learning experiences law school is meant to offer. The problem, however, arises when that competitive atmosphere is coupled with fear-based teaching techniques like cold calling, as well as stigmatization or lack of institutional support when it comes to mental health. Not only does the student's perceived stress increase, but also the competition becomes *pathological*, as the ranking or "results" of that competition start operating as a measurement for the student's external success, and more importantly, internal sense of worth.

When I was a 1L at the University of Arizona, the software we would use to apply for Biglaw during OCI clearly stated two prerequisites: you had to be in the top 25 percent **and** be on law review or on the moot court team. While these requirements will differ in law schools, my personal reality for me was that, if I didn't make it to that top, I wasn't going to stand a chance in terms of *maybe* practicing and staying in the U.S. It wasn't enough for me to just "do well" because of my immigration status. I also did not have any family or connections that could circumvent this problem. Getting to the top of the curve was not only a desire for me—it was a *literal necessity*. And a similar necessity is faced by those who have *huge* loans to pay off. The question, then, becomes: if your ability to stay, or pay off debt and make a living depends on the grades you get, what do you think you'll do?

The results from the SLSWB 2014 study[67] are insightful. Apart from corroborating an alarming alcohol-abuse pattern among fifteen law schools, the study also showed a link between the obsession with top performance and a high use of prescription drugs designed to increase concentration and alertness for longer periods of time (such as Adderall). The findings were as follows:

- 67% of the students used prescription drugs without a prescription to concentrate better while studying
- 64% did it to increase their alertness to study longer
- 49% to enhance academic performance
- 46% to increase alertness to work longer; and
- 45% to concentrate better while working.
- 20% of students reported that the reason for using prescription drugs without a prescription was to "*prevent others who also use a prescription stimulant from having an academic edge over [them].*"

67 *2014 SLSWB Study*, *supra* note 17 at 122, 135.

Remember what I told you earlier about how I went to the psychiatrist to initially get Adderall but instead was prescribed an antidepressant for OCD? Well, just as I felt I had no other option, many law students feel they have to sacrifice their mental health or obsessively compete in order to survive. And this is not just a "feeling," it's an objective reality, given the inherent competition law school fosters. In a competitive environment where the clock is ticking and the workload is increasing by the minute, it kind of makes sense that law students attempt to find ways to better compete, or at least to survive the competition they're facing.

We all know how common Adderall is in the United States and in other places, as well. It's called *Rubifen* in Spain. And to be completely honest, when you have seven or eight exams in the same month—such as I did when studying in Madrid—you cannot afford to lose one day of study. Sometimes there are situations that might call for emergency measures, but these measures are to be exceptional, short-term solutions; not *the* solution.

Paradoxically, the consumption of non-prescribed Adderall can increase anxiety in people who are not suited for it or have never been diagnosed with a disorder that warrants the prescription. In fact, long-term effects of using unprescribed Adderall include chronic anxiety, panic attacks, lack of motivation, and depression. How many lawyers do you know who continue to use Adderall or other stimulants to compete within their own law firms? That's a rhetorical question, but *if you know, you know* ;-)

The reality is that most law students obsess about grades and try to score at the top so they can have a realistic chance to secure a summer—and *good paying*—job during OCI. This in turn can create high levels of stress, which are directly linked to the academic demands, fear-of-failing and the perceived stress students experience. It is not surprising that highly competitive academic environments, such as medical school and law school give rise to psychological symptoms (yes, medical students share a very similar fate with law students).

These stress levels are especially intensified during the first semester of law school. Let's take a 1L who has just started law school. This student becomes obsessive about reaching the top, because like so many, he is already drowning in debt. This means it is not an option for him *not to* score at the top. More likely than not, this student will experience obsessive thoughts about trying to make it to the top and secure a future job to pay off his debt. "*If I don't get to the top and a job at a big or mid-size law firm, I am f*cked.*" Basically. Because that student is experiencing obsessive thoughts regarding his academic performance and subsequent employment opportunities, he will likely try to control those thoughts as well.

And here's where a maladaptive coping mechanism starts taking shape. As researchers Andy Benjamin and Connie Beck explained, this thought-control and overthinking degenerates into a cycle of distress as "this new obsessive-compulsive 'coping mechanism' will increase the need for more control, potentially generating further obsessive-compulsiveness and anger."[68] In other words, we try to control our own fear and anxiety by overthinking and overanalyzing.

Yes, yes! Welcome to Overthinking Land—*I'm still trying to get out of it.* It's like, if I have all angles figured out, I'll be safe. If I make

---

68 Connie Beck, Bruce Sales & G. Andrew Benjamin, *Lawyer Distress: Alcohol-Related Problems and Other Psychological Concerns Among a Sample of Practicing Lawyers*, 10 J.L. & HEALTH 1, 55 (1995-1996).

sure everything is perfect, I'll be safe. If I know what will happen, I'll be safe. But nope. The overthinking rarely stops because there's always more to think and analyze.

Benjamin and Beck further explained this behavioral pattern through an attorney, who has developed an obsessive need to control his fears in order to manage his client's work in the adversarial arena. This newly acquired method of control and obsessive thinking is also consistent with what early researcher James Taylor[69] explained in the 70s: that the high levels of stress law students were experiencing led them to adopt certain behaviors and traits in order to survive. If that's so, could obsessive thinking be a coping mechanism we further develop or exacerbate in law school? More on that in Pt. II - *What thinking and existing like a lawyer truly means.*

As for now, reminder:

> **Law School** = [Academic demands + stress-inducing cold calling + Gauss curve + debt + obsession w/ performance - mental health education or support] **x** [365 days **x** 3 years]

What at first seemed to be "healthy" or "optimal" stress motivating a student to do well in classes can quickly turn into pathological distress, which is unlikely to decrease if the law student has no emotional skills to cope or the awareness to seek help if needed. And, as studies show, even if law students are witnessing how their mental health is decreasing, they are not inclined to seek help. The stakes are too high to do so: the potential threat to one's credibility, academic status, bar

69 Taylor, *supra* note at 4.

admission, and employability. So, what does the student (and lawyer) normally do? Drown the stress in alcohol, or otherwise self-medicate.

The curve's impact on the law student's sense of worth

As educators and '*Incubators of Future Lawyers*,' law schools need to worry about the following: When grades are out, how will the student interiorize the results? What's the dominating narrative? How will the student make sense of it, emotionally and cognitively? Because let's face it:

> *You either win or you don't. You either make it to the top or law review, or you don't. And if you got all Bs... I mean, good luck with that...*

That tends to be the dominating narrative in law school. And is it really true? Is it really true that the future of a law student is doomed because they didn't get As? And isn't this strict mindset present since the beginning of the legal journey? From the application process/ LSAT ("*If you don't get into a top law school, you won't get a job*"), to 1L year ("*If I don't nail a cold call, that means I'm stupid*"), to grades ("*If I didn't make it to the top 10%, forget it—I won't be able to pay off my debt*") to the bar exam ("*I failed, therefore I'm useless*")? It is not uncommon to hear these narratives because the legal field frequently runs this type of strict mindset, where only extremes are considered. But where's the middle ground?

Michelle Obama failed the bar exam on her first try. So did John F. Kennedy. For real, where's the space for growth? My colleagues who are currently coaching graduates with the bar exam still report that failing the bar continues to be silenced and stigmatized. I failed the bar exam the first time, and it crushed me completely—until I realized that score didn't determine my worth. But until I came to that realization, it was *extremely painful.* And I wouldn't want my worst enemy to go through that emotional pain, or the feeling of deep unworthiness.

'Sense of worth' can be defined as the internal sense of feeling that you are good enough and worthy of love and belonging from others. In other words, it means attaching value to your being. With that in mind, let's consider some hypotheticals that would represent some of that seventy percent (70%) of law students who *did not make it to the top of the curve.*[70]

Hypothetical #1: Jack is a high-performing student who starts law school feeling pretty confident. He got mostly As in college. However, after a semester of cold calling and competition, feelings of unworthiness start kicking in. Impostor's syndrome and anxiety start running his days. The year is over and he stayed in the middle of the curve. He feels like a failure to mentors, professors, and friends. *"How is this possible? I used to be a top student. This means I am not so smart after all. I am a failure."* Unfortunately, Jack has no emotional skills to deal with all that—he has always been a top performer and has always "figured it out." He doesn't want to look weak. *How will*

70 I know I can't possibly cover all people's situations in these hypotheticals. As such, if none of these speak to you, know that your specific situation matters too. Take what resonates and leave what doesn't.

his family take that he's no longer a top student? Ashamed, he doesn't allow himself to ask for help because he's never done so in the past.

Hypothetical #2: Jose starts law school feeling resilient. He has been through a lot in his life and he is humble and compassionate. He is excited to become a lawyer. Even though he tries extremely hard, the curve is merciless and he ends up at the bottom of it. Plus, the other kids have lawyers in their families and had the resources to pay for pre-law courses before law school. He always feels he's behind. Feelings of unworthiness start kicking in, and while he knows that life is more than just law school, depression sets in because he starts getting really anxious about getting a good job as a lawyer. He knows he needs to increase that GPA or else he will not be able to pay his debt. Second semester grades are out. He did "okay," but not well enough to apply for the best-paying jobs. The "*I am not good enough*" narrative sets in. It is only after he is out of law school that he realizes how his self-esteem was affected.

Hypothetical #3: Sylvia starts law school feeling extremely excited. She doesn't really understand what the curve means; no one has explained it to her, so she just studies like she used to in college. She attends all the networking events her law school organizes because she thinks going to those is really important during her first year. However, all the time she spends in those events starts being a huge opportunity cost for her study time. Grades are out. She gets a couple of Cs. For the very first time in her entire life, she might be academically dismissed if she does not raise her GPA. She doesn't know what to do. She studied hard. She is so confused and ashamed of herself. *How is this possible? What does this mean?* She's suddenly depressed and in her head a lot.

Hypothetical #4: Anna starts law school knowing exactly what the curve means and how competitive the system is. She's done a lot of research before getting to that starting point. Her whole first year, she solely concentrates on her grades. Unconsciously, she neglects her partner and friends because "she has no time to lose." She understands she's running a "race" and that she needs to get to the top of the curve in order to win. Indeed, she makes it to the top of the curve. Law review. She does an amazing job during OCI and gets plenty of offers. Everything looks perfect from the outside. And yet, she continues to experience anxiety. The pressure of being perfect. The pressure of maintaining her grades and status. The pressure of not getting sick, ever. She's running for Law Review's Editor. There's also the clinic, the externship, and leadership positions in a couple of associations. She also needs to be perfectly prepared for class. She can't control her obsessive thinking. She must perform great at everything. She must be productive, at all times. The pressure of doing it all. By the end of her 2L year, she hits burnout and starts experiencing serious mental health symptoms.[71]

Most of these characters tend to feel some sort of depression-like symptoms and others are overly activated (anxiety). First, what most law students don't know is that they were up against a bell curve,

71 I see myself reflected in here (not in everything, but definitely in the pressure of being at the top, constantly). I was lucky that I had committed to doing yoga and using therapy as I was going through all of it; otherwise I don't think I would have made it.

and that the difference between a B+ and a A- could have just been a point, a word, a slightly better structure. If the student does not understand these parameters, they will most likely blame themselves because the unconscious message they receive from the law school institution is that *grades determine their value in front of employers.* But in reality, grades do not determine their worth as human beings or potential as future lawyers.

Moreover, if law school itself embraces this type of competition and elitism, without giving any weight to a student's humanity or other skills that are not necessarily measured by a curve, chances are the student will adapt to that way of detrimental thinking. And yes, grades can determine job opportunities but they do not determine a student's worth. There are other ways and other avenues to succeed as a lawyer. *And the 70 percent of law students who might not feel like "top" law students deserve to know that truth.*

If your grades weren't great, you might have a harder time finding a job. But you know what? You'll have the opportunity to master other skills—namely, street-smart skills. These include picking yourself up from the floor when you fall or feel unworthy. When you feel beaten up. When you feel that you don't have a choice. And yet, you stand up and keep fighting. That skill, also known as *resilience,* is also a pretty good one when you enter the legal world. And what about social skills? The ones required to get clients? Or the business skills required to start and run a law firm? How about creative thinking or *reaaaal* good writing? How about emotional intelligence to manage the ups and downs of being a lawyer? Success as an attorney is about so much more than one's law school grades, and legal education has yet to embrace that hidden side of the equation.

4

[Institutionalized] Stigmatization of Mental Health Struggles

"... Mental health is a neglected issue for law students."

— Response from a law student *in* Ian Ayres et al., *Anxiety Psychoeducation for Law Students: A Pilot Program*, 67 J. LEG. EDUCATION 118, 134 (2017).

I often see a dissonance between the current stated interest of law firms (or, at least, what their marketing efforts say) in emotional well-being/mental health and their continued glorification of machine-like behaviors.[72] In other words, we are starting to care about mental health in the legal field, and yet, we're still operating with the same expectations of perfection and machine-like behaviors that cause our mental health to suffer in the first place. A similar dissonance takes place in most law schools. While the mental health conversation is starting to gain some momentum, students continue to be reluctant to talk or open up about their struggles. Why?

In law school, students experience a collective fear of being perceived as weak (let alone, mentally ill). This fear translates into students not feeling safe about any type of mental health issue they might be going through. Covertly crafted as a defense mechanism to survive a highly-competitive environment, performing as a *perfect* law student simply becomes a necessary trait to qualify as "good material" when it comes to hiring and networking in the legal jungle. Interestingly, this superficial appearance is not something that law students suddenly—and voluntarily—decide to adopt when they start law school. Rather, they're unconsciously "encouraged" to do so. Do *I*, as a law student, want to be seen by my peers and professors as someone who might have anxiety or depression?

---

72 For example, a 2022 Report on the State of the Legal Market showed how attorney turnover had hit record levels in 2021, with law firms close to losing one-quarter of their associates—regardless of significant salary increases designed to retain them. Thomson Reuters Institute, *2022 Report on the State of the Legal Market* (2022), 2-4 https://www.thomsonreuters.com/en-us/posts/wp-content/uploads/sites/20/2022/01/State-of-Legal-Market-Report_Final.pdf.

Law students' reluctance to ask for help

The *Suffering in Silence* Survey (i.e., the 2014 SLSWB Study) was the first study to gather empirical information as to *why* law students were not seeking help for mental health issues or drug-abuse problems. These were the top reasons when it came to not seeking help for substance abuse - mental health problems:

- Potential threat to bar admission [63% - 45% of students]
- Potential threat to job or academic status [62% - 48% of students]
- Social stigma [43% - 47% of students]
- Concerns about privacy [43% - 30% of students]
- Financial reasons [41% - 47% of students]
- The belief that they could handle the problem themselves [39% - 36% of students]
- Not having the time to seek help [36% - 34% of students]

Moreover, 43% of respondents admitted that, "if [they] had a mental health problem, [their] chances of getting admitted to the bar are better if the problem is hidden."[73] Likewise, Yale Law's Report on Mental Health showed that a high percentage of Yale law students feared exclusion and stigma from a variety of actors, including faculty, peers, and staff, as well as the state bar association or the Lawyer Assistance Program.

73 *2014 SLSWB Study, supra* note 17, at 141, 142. Moreover, 49% of all respondents indicated that if they had a drug or alcohol problem, their chances of getting admitted to the bar were also better if hidden. *Id.* at 142.

I mean, what would you do? Imagine being in a law school environment where everyone is acting like everything is fine, where mental health is not talked about, where there are barely any mental health resources to get help without you paying more money or losing study time; and where having mental health problems are sort of a turn-off for future employers or a threat to your future as a lawyer (in fact, many states continue to have Character and Fitness applications that ask mental health questions that can directly disqualify a person from becoming a lawyer). Hence, it makes sense not to ask for help where there is no real support system to *support* you.

Law students' mental struggles mirror their future struggles as lawyers

As I embarked on this research, I felt I had found the *Philosopher's Stone*[74] when I read the following sentence from the 1994 Report of the AALS (Special Committee on Problems of Substance abuse in Law Schools):

The seeds of substance abuse in lawyers may be sown in law school.[75]

I still need to pause when I read this because one may ask: isn't there a pretty strong correlation between the data on law students' mental health and lawyers' mental health? Or, rephrasing the

74 In Western culture, the philosopher's stone was believed to be an unknown substance sought by alchemists for its ability to transform base metals into precious ones, such as gold and silver. Alchemists also believed that the elixir of life could be derived from this stone.

75 Association of American Law Schools Comm. Report, *Report of the AALS Special Committee on the Problem of Substance Abuse in Law School,* 44 J. Legal Educ. 35-80 (1994).

question: why are lawyers three times more likely to suffer from depression than any other profession?

The legal profession has historically believed that emotions clouded our rational thinking as lawyers;[76] and therefore, we have tried to eradicate the emotional humanity—and struggles—from our profession. Or, in other words, we have stigmatized any type of mental health struggle. We have done so for centuries because it represented a liability to our status. And since it's a liability, let's eradicate it completely. But such eradication is impossible, because apart from being lawyers, we're also humans, which means that we suffer in life, just like everybody else. We feel. We love and we get hurt. We experience frustration. Conflict, grief, unworthiness. We experience sadness. Fear. And so on. And this happens even when we're wearing our black suits, yes.

For example, a 2016 study[77]on lawyer impairment surveyed almost 13,000 licensed attorneys and examined alcohol use, substance abuse, mental health, and help-seeking behaviors. These were some of the results:

- 19% of lawyers suffered from severe anxiety.
- 20.6% of lawyers screened positive for hazardous or harmful and potentially alcohol-dependent drinking.
- 23% suffered from significant symptoms of stress.
- 28% experienced significant symptoms of depression.

---

76 Part II deals more in depth with lawyer stereotypes from the 19th century as well as how the legal mind operates.

77 Patrick R. Krill et. al, *The Prevalence of Substance Use and Other Mental Concerns Among American Attorneys*, 10 J. Addiction Medicine 46, 50, 51 (2016).

- 11.5% had suicidal thoughts in the previous year, noting to have considered suicide as a potential solution to their issues.

If a student learns in law school that seeking help is a threat to his status/worthiness, work or employability, do you really think that he will suddenly become enlightened on mental health support when he becomes a lawyer? Or would he rather continue this reluctance to seek help, just as he did in law school? A rhetorical question, but you know what I'm getting at. Even though things seem to start changing, the legal field continues to glorify the *machine-like lawyer* who is not bothered by *anyone or anything*. We continue to glorify the lack of emotions. We continue to act like "everything is fine." We continue to glorify long hours with no sleep and "sucking it up." We continue to embrace this illusion of perfection in our lawyer persona, because our other side—the one dealing with emotions, mental health, and our humanity—represents a weakness to us. We erroneously believe that our emotional—yet human—side constitutes a liability *per se*. Accordingly, we hide our mental health struggles in order to protect our perfect, glorified, lawyer persona. And can you blame us? How else can a person survive in a highly competitive environment where emotions are seen as weakness or a loss of machine-like productivity?

But more importantly, is this the type of emotionless education we want law students to interiorize? When law schools do not value mental health or embrace human vulnerability (authentically, not just theoretically by adding one therapist on staff and a couple of sentences on their websites), law students will interiorize such limitations and integrate them as part of the game's "rules." They will adopt the following mantra: "Mental health struggles *equals* weakness, and therefore, reduced employability." This is the message they will leave with and that is the culture they will bring into their law firms. And for those of us who are attorneys already, we know this message does not get easier on us as we progress in our legal careers. After we've hidden our pain (so that our colleagues don't know we're struggling, of course) and after we've done so consistently, for years, we arrive at a crossroads.

We either cope with alcohol/drugs, or medication and intense therapy; or we end up leaving the profession in the traditional sense (if debt allows for that route, of course). And because law students can't leave law school (*reminder: they are now drowning in debt*), they are frequently left with just one option: hide the problem and simply cope with alcohol or any other temporarily-helpful drug or medication. Is that a proper foundation for the future generation of lawyers, judges, public defenders, legislators?

If we don't want law students—or future lawyers—to dehumanize themselves in their practice; that is, hide their mental health struggles, we need to normalize the fact that lawyers are also emotional beings, who may, at times, suffer, too. We need to find healthier ways to *exist* as lawyers in this world. And to do that, we first need to deconstruct outdated lawyer stereotypes and ways of *lawyer thinking* that prove detrimental to our bodies and minds. That is what the next section is all about.

Part ii

•

What thinking & existing as a lawyer truly means

*

Though we're in the 21st century, most law schools continue to operate and embrace a lawyer stereotype that was created in the 19th century. This created persona tends to be a non-emotional high-performer who is highly rational, perfectionistic and always adversarial in his strategy to win the case. This persona is generally a 24/7 machine-like worker with no vulnerabilities or need for breaks—because breaks cut into billing and productivity. And even though this lawyer stereotype no longer fits in the 21st century, the modern law student is still forced into that stereotype. In addition, recurrent negative hypothetical thinking and perfectionism places law students and lawyers in a collective illusive reality, where unreasonable standards of (non-existent) perfection must always be reached.

There are also hidden narratives within the legal field that have proven detrimental to our success as professionals and human beings. The fact that asking for support or help may be seen as a sign of weakness—or incompetence—is connected to this false illusion of perfection that we continue to unconsciously perpetuate. Likewise, not showing vulnerability due to fear of judgment is connected with institutional rigidity. Take, for example, the Bar's character & fitness applications on mental health, or other covert processes that dehumanize lawyers who are, in the end, penalized for not conforming to certain gender identities and dynamics.

We are not these non-emotional, only rational thinkers, who are able to work 24/7 without an eye blink. We are not this "perfect" lawyer persona that will never miss a call, get sick for more than five days in a row, forget to reply to an important email, have a family emergency, experience depression, or make any type of human mistake. Moreover, some of us prefer not to be aggressive when dealing with or going up against our colleagues. We are also not legal machines. We never were. We're humans, like everybody else. We experience anxiety and grief. We have emotions, like everybody else.

As such, why are law schools still embracing an outdated lawyer persona within their institutions? Given the serious mental health crisis in the legal field, don't we know any better by now? To tackle these points in more depth, Part II covers the following:

Chapter 5 · The [19th Century] Lawyer Identity; and
Chapter 6 · The Legal Mind: A New Way of Thinking and Seeing the World.

5

The [19th Century] Lawyer Identity

The popular image of lawyers is that we are committed to formal rationality. We are trained to cabin 'empathic' responses and remain steadfast in our commitment to legal principles despite emotional dissonance.

—Toni Massaro, *Empathy, Legal Storytelling, and the Rule of Law: New Words, Old Wounds?* 87 MICH. L. REV. 2099, 2103 (1989)[78]

78 Professor Massaro was my Constitutional Law Professor at the University of Arizona · James E. Rogers College of Law. She is one of the exceptions I mentioned earlier, and in my experience, she never used the fear-based teaching techniques this book talks about; to the very contrary, she used enthusiasm to inspire her law students to *think* more creatively.

At the time the institution of law school was starting to emerge—that is, around the 18th century—we didn't know much about neuroscience, emotional intelligence, or how we somatize our stress and emotions. As such, the law school system was created to only nourish the "rational" and "intellectual" sides of a lawyer. A successful lawyer was someone who was completely detached from his emotions because it was thought these could cloud his thinking. That successful lawyer was also *always* prepared to endure any and all forms of stress and he (often a white male)[79] generally had no real family obligations because his wife stayed at home with the kids.[80]

Always relegated to the office and to the thinking realms, this lawyer persona was highly rational, barely expressed any emotions, made no mistakes, and was always ready to attack the other side—*zealously*. Moreover, that lawyer did not like anything that wasn't science-based or fact-based, as that always decreased the probability of truth and certainty. Finally, that persona was almost always serious, formal and seemed to have everything under control. Without exception, that lawyer persona always worked very, very long hours.

Roughly, that was the lawyer stereotype we saw in real life, and the one that was consistently portrayed on Television (TV). And yes, I am getting a little cynical here, but do you see where I am going? That's our profession—in real life and on TV. We ignore the simple fact that, regardless of perfection-like standards and billing requirements, we are also human beings and therefore we feel emotions and go through the pain of life as well. In this chapter, we'll go through

79 The American Bar Association explicitly denied black people membership until 1950.

80 Women didn't get admitted to the American Bar Association until 1918.

several of the constructed identities that we continue to perpetuate in our field, including:

- The **"only rational, non-emotional, machine-like"** lawyer
- The **"perfect in all tasks"** lawyer
- The **"highly productive and busy"** lawyer
- The **"24/7 available, never gets sick, no time off"** lawyer
- The **"zealous, win-at-all-costs"** lawyer

We'll also dissect other less obvious but hidden narratives in the field, such as those of the submissive or gender-conforming lawyer.

The "only-rational, non-emotional, machine-like" lawyer

One of my best friends from law school recently quit her job at a big law firm in New York. Last year, while she was still at the job, we scheduled one of our catch-ups over Zoom. As we started talking, she mentioned how a partner in her team had just tragically died that morning. I urgently asked how she was feeling emotionally. She replied she was simply in shock, as the whole team had held a meeting later that day and the death of the partner had barely been discussed, even though everybody knew him. In an attempt to lessen the heaviness of her situation, we cynically joked about how, per law firm culture, the sudden death of a person in your team does not necessarily result in automatic rescheduling of a work meeting—let alone allow for the rest of the day off, maybe to honor any grief the tragic event might have created in the team!

But ain't that really messed up?

Even though we momentarily laughed, my friend was deeply sad and, in an environment, where that natural sadness was not acknowledged, validated, or legitimized. How long can one work at a place that pushes aside the basic human experience of tragedy, sadness, and grief? In the legal field, emotions are often seen as a weakness. Apart from the clear fact that emotional overwhelm can interfere with billing, emotions also interfere with perfection—that is, the notion of not having anything that could distract the lawyer from reaching maximum productivity. Just like a powerful computer competing to mine the maximum amount of bitcoins, you know? In fact, burnout or disease must manifest physically in order for the firm to take you seriously; an emotional manifestation of a mental health struggle is generally neglected.

Moreover, emotions have historically constituted a liability because they could interfere with the lawyer's commitment to pure rationality. Hence why law schools have repeatedly placed an exclusive, institutional emphasis on objective thought, rational deduction and empirical proof.[81] In the world's eyes, lawyers are "thinkers" rather than "feelers." But is that really true?

Apart from the obvious gap that exists between the popular lawyer's identity (as a non-emotional being) and the real identity in the lawyer's real life (as an individual with emotions), there is one thing we know for sure: emotions are part of our human fabric, whether we're lawyers or not. Neuroscience shows us that emotions

81 Benjamin, *supra* note 6 at 246 (citing M. Meltsner, *Feeling Like a Lawyer*, 33 J. LEGAL EDUC. 624, 633 (1983).

are necessary in all of our decision-making processes. For example, as a part of my training at the Google-born Search Inside Yourself Institute,[82]we discussed a scenario where a patient had undergone surgery for a brain tumor.

While the patient's surgery had been successful, the surgeons accidentally cut—and damaged—the connection between the amygdala and the prefrontal cortex. As a quick neurology refresher, the amygdala is our center for emotional processes, memories, and danger-detection; and our prefrontal cortex (PFC) is the region in charge of our executive functions, and more complex cognitive behavior, personality expression, decision-making, and social behavior. The amygdala and the PFC are connected and closely work together. In simpler terms, when the amygdala signals a threat or a stressful situation, the PFC helps the person regulate what she is sensing.

Therefore, the existence of that relationship helps us identify, regulate, and prioritize emotions. But when that relationship has been severed, we lose the ability to do so, which is what happened to the patient whose connection between his amygdala and his PCF had been damaged. He suddenly struggled with making decisions. Quite literally, he no longer had the ability to regulate, identify, and prioritize emotions when making a decision.

Apart from this scientific argument, is it even ethical to strip lawyers from their emotions? How are lawyers, as "rational thinkers,"

82 The Search Inside Yourself Leadership Institute (SIYLI) is a non-profit organization that offers mindfulness-based emotional intelligence training programs rooted in neuroscience and organizational psychology. The organization was founded in 2012 by Chade-Meng Tan, a former engineer at Google. SIYLI's trainings are designed to help people develop the skills of emotional intelligence, mindfulness, and leadership.

expected to *not* have emotions affect them? Isn't that the equivalent of dehumanizing them, a little?

What's interesting is that we also experience a contradiction within our own work, as Toni Massaro noted. While "we are trained to cabin 'empathic' responses and remain steadfast in our commitment to legal principles despite emotional dissonance," we are at the same time expected to be empathic and caring attorneys for our client's causes. Okay, so wait. We're expected to be empathic when dealing with our clients but such empathy should not affect our rational capacity—not even a bitty bit. I mean, do you truly think we can switch our emotional responses on and off, just like that?

Brené Brown explains that there is no such a thing as selective numbing.[83] We cannot selectively numb specific parts of an emotion, as if we are sorting through our favorite candy. Given the full spectrum of our human emotions, when we numb the 'negative' ones, we also numb the positive ones. So under that logic, if an attorney is forced to numb his empathy in order to remain "completely rational" in his work, he is also counterintuitively numbing the good empathy as well (which, by the way, is the one that is beneficial for his clients, colleagues, and loved ones). This pattern of numbing emotions can certainly affect a person's life, soul, and mental health.

Furthermore, law students are trained to eradicate or hide any type of emotional dissonance when representing a client. That is, they are somewhat expected to turn into an only-logical, legal machine. As the student (or young lawyer) identifies the full spectrum of her client's case, law school teaches her that, in order to win, she

---

83 Brené Brown, Daring Greatly: How the Courage to Be Vulnerable Transforms the Way We Live, Love, Parent, and Lead (Gotham Books, 2012).

is also expected to disregard her own moral values, empathies, and feelings about the case for the sake of her client's victory.

For example, let's hypothetically dive into Sylvia's life, a passionate public defender. Sylvia has always been a humanist and a social justice-oriented advocate. She believes everybody deserves a trial and a second chance in life. This notion of justice is deeply embedded in her heart, since way before she started law school. On Monday, Sylvia gets a case where the accused, a twenty-ish year-old boy (along with his friends) drugged a younger girl and raped her. As a lawyer, Sylvia knows that she can win her case, misinterpreting consent or breaking into some of the required elements for rape. There are ways to get this guy off the hook. She knows she can make it work.

What we don't see is that Sylvia was once drugged and raped as a teenager. Therefore, the inner Sylvia knows drugging and raping girls is often a *modus operandi* among rapists, who tend to repeat their conduct. She can also sense that the victim is probably not the first or the last one that this group of friends will assault. But none of this matters. She is not allowed to let it matter. She must defend her client.

Legal education cannot realistically support Sylvia's emotional and cognitive dissonance, which is why we attempt to construct legal thought as a rights-oriented philosophy. This means that, as lawyers, we must always focus on the client's rights, and subordinate our emotional reactions to our client's rights. Our emotional dissonance can never interfere, or at a minimum, it remains unimportant because the priority is to win the case. As Susan Dacoiff explains, a lawyer is always taught to remain in an "emotionally neutral state in order to be an advocate."[84] But is this a feasible expectation? How will Sylvia process the confusion, triggers, and emotional pain she is feeling internally? How can she integrate her values if she cannot begin to accept those out in the open?

But again, that doesn't matter. What will matter is whether she wins the case. The more detached she is from her emotions, the better. Now, is this healthy in the long-term? We'll keep talking about this in *Chapter 7 · Redefining & Humanizing the Lawyer Identity.*

The "perfect" lawyer

The first thing a law student learns in law school is that the legal profession requires perfection. This is so because the ethical rules require it: a good lawyer is expected to be correct and accurate in legal tasks. Lawyers must have an in-depth understanding of the law and of the other side's position. As such, law students are taught that a good lawyer must be able to take in *and* understand great amounts of information, both from his client's scenario as well as his opponent's; and, in doing so, he must be extremely detail-oriented, as missing a key factor can change the outcome of a case. The Rules of Professional Conduct emphasize something like:

> "A lawyer's workload must be controlled so that each matter can be handled competently."[85]

---

84 Susan Daicoff, *Lawyer, Know Thyself: A Review of Empirical Research on Attorney Attributes Bearing on Professionalism*, 45 Am. U. L. Rev. 1337, 1401 (1997) (citations omitted). *See also* Comments [1] and [2] to Rule 1.1, Model Rules of Prof'l Conduct R. 1.1 (2020).

85 Model Rules of Prof'l Conduct R. 1.5 (2020) (emphasis added).

Okay, that is understandable. There are, however, three things to consider here. One, lawyers may have hundreds of matters (i.e., cases). Two, this high level of performance or perfection is expected in a combative, adversarial arena. And three, there is a difference between never missing a deadline and internalizing perfectionism as a form of living. I will go into it in more depth.

First, law students—and lawyers—are expected to multitask a huge workload and become effective problem-solvers in *every single situation* they encounter, which often results in a higher standard of perfection than the average person because they cannot—or are not expected—to make any mistakes in any of those situations. Second, lawyers are expected to achieve perfection in non-supportive environments.

For example, Elienne Zimmerman wrote an *incredible* piece in the New York Times titled *The Lawyer, the Addict,*[86] and she touched upon the relationship between the lawyers' expectation to reach perfection *within* the hostile reality of the field:

> . . . Wil Miller, who . . . spent 10 years as a sex crimes prosecutor, the last six months of which he was addicted to methamphetamines, [explained that] 'being a surgeon is stressful, for instance—but not in the same way. It would be like having another surgeon across the table from you trying to undo your operation. In law, you are financially rewarded for being hostile.[87]

---

86 I highly recommend this piece (and story) to any law student, lawyer, and their loved ones. Heartfelt, raw, insightful, and beautifully-written.

87 Elienne Zimmerman, T*he Lawyer, the Addict,* N.Y. Times, (July 15, 2017), https://www.nytimes.com/2017/07/15/business/lawyers-addiction-mental-health.html.

In other words, you're trying to be perfect and the other lawyer is trying to destroy that perfection.

Finally, when something is done repeatedly, it can solidify as a new habit or way of thinking—as neuroscience teaches us. For example, when I was a very young child, my father, a civil engineer (and sort of a math genius when he was younger), would repeatedly scream at me when I would make the common mistakes of a seven-year old as she is trying to be perfect in the resolution of an equation, but more importantly, in her dad's eyes. At that moment, in my little head, I "understood" that I wasn't good at math and that there was no way for me to ever be good at it. Once I became a teenager, I told my dad I did not want him to teach me math anymore, and little by little, I started hating the subject.[88] And no, I didn't study law because of this. I had always wanted to become a lawyer; and as a current appellate lawyer, I cherish the analytical—and creative—process behind the development of arguments, and, eventually, the writing of the final brief. And while my dad—also an incredibly devoted and loving one—didn't know any better about teaching

88 As an anecdote, one of my mentors and Torts Professor at the U of A—Jane Bambauer, J.D. & B.S. in Mathematics at Yale—once told me that law is like pure math. I will never forget the day where she started explaining the cost-benefit analysis formula. And yes, science people will say *please, that's not math*—but it was a formula, so please be kind... During class, my body suddenly froze; my breath shortened. And I thought to myself: *that's it, I won't be able to get an A now. I won't be able to make law review. I won't be able to stay in the US.* I went to her office hours that day, and for whatever reason, felt safe enough to tell her about my little "math trauma." She supported me and reminded me of how insightful and witty my contributions had been throughout the semester, and how that experience did not determine my intelligence. Then as finals approached, a loving classmate named Amanda sat down with me to review the formula; and did so with the ingredients of a great teacher: *patience and compassion*. Once the fall semester came to an end, I had ended up at the top in Torts, with an A, and later becoming a teaching fellow for other 1L students.

methods (mainly because he had been raised during a dictatorship where it was acceptable to teach with fear), my main point is this:

> *Enforcing perfectionism—or any type of fixed mindset—can have serious psychological implications in someone's life and career.*[89]

When we are not taught how to be self-compassionate in those moments where we do not reach perfection right away, we become trapped in a fixed, black-and-white type of thinking. More dangerously, we learn that only if we are [legally] perfect in *everything* we do in law, will we be "worthy" and rewarded in the profession. But as soon as we make a mistake, that illusion of perfection will vanish—and so will our competence and sense of worth.

The inevitable reality is that, at some point, someday, we will make a mistake.[90] And that is because making mistakes is an integral part of being human. Maybe it won't be a dramatic mistake, and just a couple of non-perfect bluebook citations in an important brief before a federal circuit court, but the point is that the merciless lawyer self-criticism will kick in, fiercely—especially if the person has not developed effective mechanisms to understand that a mistake does not define their worth.

---

89 And though I've healed a significant part of my perfectionism or black-or-white thinking, writing it on paper still hurts and it makes me feel very vulnerable. However, I know that there will be at least one reader who will feel seen with my story. And that for me is enough reason to be vulnerable, even if it triggers the heck out of me – not gonna lie!

90 And yes, as a lawyer, this sentence terrifies me as well—believe me. Every day I practice switching from a fixed mindset to a growth one (keep reading), and I have a feeling it's going to take me a lifetime to finally accept that perfection doesn't exist, and that what I do is always good enough. So if you're in that process, I'm right there with you.

In this regard, Carol Dweck is a Stanford psychologist whose research focuses on the difference between fixed and growth mindsets. She defines a fixed mindset, or black-and-white thinking, as follows:

> In a fixed mindset, people believe their basic qualities, like their intelligence or talent, are simply fixed traits. They spend their time documenting[91] their intelligence or talent instead of developing them.[92]

Dweck goes on to explain that people with fixed mindsets believe that they're either smart or dumb, and that there is no way to change this. Accordingly, any indicators or proof of this—such as a B grade in law school, not making it to the top of the curve, or not having a strong argument at a given moment—simply confirms the belief that they're either dumb, or that they are less intelligent than they thought. This is exactly what happens with law students when they receive *Bs* after getting *As* throughout their college experience or when they freeze during a cold call—as the testimonies and studies in Part I showed us. Unfortunately, fixed mindsets have been reinforced since our early experiences in school—as there is normally a rigid distinction between the good students *versus* the bad students.

Under this fixed or black-and-white logic, law school (and by consequence, our legal profession) also revolves around the idea that we're either perfect law students and lawyers—or we're not. We see that play out through the grading curve, cold calling, rankings,

---

91 I interpret "documenting" as the typical trajectory of us *overachievers*...

92 Carol Dweck, Mindset: The New Psychology of Success (Random House Publishing Group, 2007).

and so on. How many law students lose their sense of worth after first semester grades are out? How many law students have a mental breakdown because they think those grades speak about their potential as attorneys and as human beings? How many law students' sense of worth shifts because they were not "perfect" during their cold calls? How many lawyers enter a depression because a judge rules against their motion, or they lose a trial, or their client complains about them?

If we don't teach students a growth mindset[93]or how to deal with perfectionism, chances are they will simply internalize the following *unspoken* law school rules:

- *Your grades end up determining how good you truly are as a lawyer because that's what the legal industry truly values.*

- *If you didn't nail the cold call, then you aren't as smart as you thought; otherwise, you would have nailed it.*

- *If you don't make it to law review, you are not good enough in the legal world; or at least, not as smart as you thought.*

- *If you didn't make it to the top 10%, got the clerkship or the Biglaw job, then you're also not good enough; but kind of mediocre, instead.*

- *Work and assignments always override your emotions or mental health because remember, you're competing against equally*

93 We'll dive even more deeply into growth mindsets in Part III, so please keep reading along ;)

smart lawyers – and this basically means you don't have time to get sick or sad because those problems will lower your chances of winning.

- *Finally, if you let emotions take over or let stress affect your work, this just means you're not cut out for this profession to begin with.*

Do you see your younger or current self in any of these examples? These law school-related narratives are, again, another illustration of what a fixed mindset looks like. With no room for growth or progress, we are stuck with a feeling that we fail if we do not reach some made-up definition of perfection. If we have a slip, an emotional breakdown, a moment of not being in our 150%, then we're just not as good as we thought. For law students—and given the competition in law school—this anxiety does not just stay in the realm of grades; it continues on to the internships or clerkships their peers got and they did not. Does this competition and endless search for external signs of our worthiness[94] ever stop? Do we ever get a break from having to be perfect in front of clients, colleagues, judges, family? If we live our lives under this type of mindset, how do you think we'll interpret the common human experience of failing?

Whether it's that article you want to submit for publication but you're unsure if it's good enough, that email you sent to the client and forgot to mention "X" detail, that job you want to apply for but you're not sure your qualifications are strong enough, that hobby or

94 Simply picture a lawyer looking at another lawyer's website or resume and suddenly enter a stage of *comparisonitis* or impostor's syndrome.

skill you want to learn but you can't bear the fact that you won't be good at it first… Truthfully, I ask you (and myself): how many times during the day do you expect perfection out of yourself?

Sí, the struggle is real.

The "highly productive" lawyer

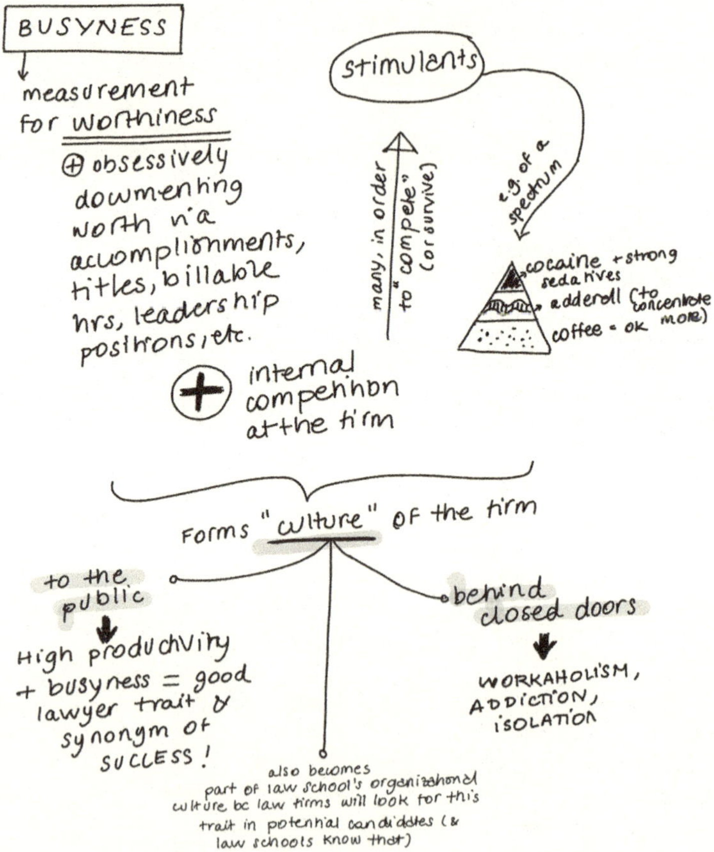

The lawyer persona is always *busy*—isn't it?

It is very important to understand the cycle behind this specific stereotype, especially because of its connection to workaholism and the use of stimulants. First, as lawyers, we attach a significant part of our worthiness to our level of busyness. If we're not being productive, we're likely feeling guilty—so we'll fill in the gaps with things to do, committees to sign up for, and so on. This behavior shows up because the busier we are, the more we're accomplishing according to our psyche. As most of us are overachievers, we're collecting (or obsessively documenting) accomplishments, titles, certifications, and "wins." The thing is, we believe that it is *that* list of accomplishments that will determine whether we're successful or not; in other words, whether we're finally good enough or not.

> *College degree? LSAT score? Law school ranking? Class ranking? Law review or moot competition? Clinic work? Any young lawyer award? Committee positions? and the typical... Wait, what college did you go to? What law school did you go to? At what firm do you work at? Ohhh, okay.*

Typical lawyer questions. We're just trying to filter and figure out if the established hierarchical system says you're good enough—or not. But when it comes to busyness and workaholism, the dangerous thing is that neither of them has an expiration date or an acceptance letter from an institution. Rather, we can seek more and more of it, indefinitely. Guided by an internal desire to achieve recognition, external validation, and 'worthiness' within the field, we enter the overachiever hamster wheel. Some use it to achieve; others to escape their personal lives. The problem is this: if one day, for whatever reason, that wheel stops moving —our identity and sense of worth will suddenly collapse. Why? Because our worthiness was placed at the center of it.

In the legal field, busyness and high productivity is seen as a *great* trait. When I say high productivity, I am not talking about the healthy kind—with boundaries and so on—I am talking about disguised workaholism or high-functioning anxiety. Note, however, that busyness and high productivity must go together. If you're highly productive in your tasks, but are not too busy, that's a red flag in the field. A "good lawyer" needs to have both because there's so much competition around him! Competition dictates that you cannot let your guard down, for if you do, your busyness and productivity might not be good enough. See?

This is basically the moment when in order to compete, keep up or survive, our coffee consumption suddenly starts going up. Then we realize that we need more focus and concentration to be able to keep up with the workload, so maybe we consider taking Adderall or something that increases our capacity for lengthy concentration—just for a little bit, you know? After that, well—some might end up going from prescription amphetamines (Adderall) to street stimulants (methamphetamine or cocaine).

Lisa F. Smith, a former NY Big Law[95] associate—who bravely shared her story of cocaine addiction in the Washington Post—tells us about some of the intricacies behind that "busyness" stereotype

95 There are obviously differences between the private sector, different sized firms, as well as the public sector; but a similar pattern keeps emerging: *busyness always equals success*. For example, why is it accepted or considered completely normal for lawyers to work on weekends?

that looks so cool on TV, when Mike and Harvey Specter (from the TV show *Suits*) are at the office at 10 pm, on a Saturday:

> Top law firms are filled with academic overachievers who are realizing their dreams when they start work. Upon arrival, though, instead of making a brilliant argument before a judge, these young lawyers may find themselves competing with the similarly gifted peers for the privilege of proofreading documents for a high-ranking partner. If they do a great job, they may get to proofread all weekend. That's what success can look like. . . Over the years, I have known lawyers with eating disorders, out-of-control shopping habits and extreme exercise addictions.[96]

She further notes:

> Given the intensity and demands of the legal profession, it's not surprising that lawyers turn to stimulants. Like me, lawyers I knew fueled their late night and early morning efforts with cocaine and other drugs. While there is no reliable data on the use of doctor-prescribed stimulants, such as Adderall, Vyvanse and Concerta, among lawyers, the soaring rate of prescriptions for stimulants generally and their widespread availability from drug dealers is telling.

96 Lisa F. Smith, *The Most Terrifying Part of my Drug Addiction? That My Law Firm Would Find Out*, The Washington Post (March 2016), www.washingtonpost.com ("More than 20 years ago, I became an associate at a big New York City firm and almost simultaneously spiraled into alcoholism and drug addiction").

And this makes so much sense because the same thing happens in law school. As discussed in various chapters throughout this book, the 2014 SLSWB study[97] showed a link between the obsession with top performance and the use of stimulants or prescription drugs that were known to increase concentration and alertness to study for longer periods of time. Paradoxically, the consumption of non-prescribed Adderall increases anxiety and its long-term effects can include panic attacks, lack of motivation and depression. Not that cocaine will yield better results, of course. Likewise, the 2016 study on the prevalence of substance use,[98] noted that apart from having drinking problems that traced back to law school, lawyers also found stimulants to be especially appealing given the high demands and intensity of their work. So, here are a couple of rhetorical questions for us to ponder:

> *What does a law student do when he has an insane workload over a prolonged period of time? What will he do when he realizes that not only does he need to deal with that workload, but also compete against everybody else? Most importantly, if that law student decided to take Adderall to keep up with it, do you think he will stop consuming it when he starts to practice—that is, when the workload and the stakes get even higher?*

I mean, our profession can get so unhealthy that we have to turn to non-prescribed or prescribed medication (or even illegal drugs) to survive. That happens to be the reality—not for all, but for many.

97 *2014 SLSWB Study, supra* note 17.

98 Krill et al., *supra* note 77.

And that "many" is enough reason to re-evaluate the roots of the problem, including the stereotypes that are contributing to one of the most unhealthy and stressful professions in the world.

Workaholism is a "good trait" in the eyes of law firms because the legal field glorifies it. It equals billing. It equals competition. It equals "money, success, prestige." As such, the legal field rewards candidates who exhibit that good trait. What's sad is that law schools know this, and as the main producers or incubators of those potential candidates, they train their students accordingly. Moreover, law schools have an incentive to somehow foster "workaholism" because law firms directly look for students who have this trait; and more hired students means better rankings, which eventually leads to more money.

There is a reason why law school's workload significantly differs from college. Law students are given incredible—and often insane—amounts of information to read and absorb (within a very limited amount of time) because that is what the field will expect from them. Some law schools think that what they're doing is preparing law students for the "real world"—just as my dad thought he was preparing me for the real world when he was being overly strict and rigid with my education; when in reality, what I needed were the emotional skills to navigate and find meaning in life. The difference is that my dad—and so many other parents—didn't know any better. Law schools *do* know better. Decades of data. Decades of studies. Percentages. Law students and lawyers screaming the words: *mental health.* And yet, nobody listens. How many more suicides does the legal field need to witness? How many more juicy yet heartbreaking law firm stories of addiction and burnout do we need to read? When are we going to stop the madness?

As Zimmerman noted in her story behind her ex-husband's suicide:

> Academics often study law students because students are considered a bellwether for the profession. 'They are the canaries in the coal mine,' Dr. Benjamin said. Wil Miller, the lawyer and former methamphetamine addict, said that in his experience, law school encouraged students to take emotions out of their decisions. "When you start reinforcing that with grades and money, you're not just suppressing your emotions," he said. "You are fundamentally changing who you are." Research studying lawyers' happiness supports this notion. "The psychological factors seen to erode during law school are the very factors most important to the well-being of lawyers" . . .[99]

We need to stop this glorification of busyness and workaholism in law school, and in our field. That lawyer identity produces a seemingly proud, successful person on the outside—and a deeply depressed human being, whose humanity has been stripped away, on the inside. The more he works, the more praise he gets. The more he bills, the more praise he gets. And if he can get to the machine-like level of a person who will surely sign up for a million things and accomplish each one, all the better. That lawyer will be seen as "successful," even if he has lost contact with his emotions, his

99 Zimmerman, *supra* note 87.

partner, his family, his hobbies, and the people he loves in his life. According to the field, what matters is *how much he can accomplish and produce*, like a legal machine. The rest is irrelevant.

This is the dynamic that has been perpetuated over centuries in the legal profession—and it's about damn time we break it.

The "no breaks, never gets sick, 24/7 available" lawyer

One of the things we used to joke about in law school is that you "didn't have time to die" because there was so much reading to do. In the real, legal world, you can't either—or at least know that if you get sick for more than a week, your promotion or career might suffer. Another common lawyer identity is that lawyer who barely takes a vacation (which is widely accepted in society).

If you google the words "lawyers' vacation" together, you'll get articles like: '*Law Firms Should Consider Mandatory Vacation Policies*' [abovethelaw.com], '*Tips for Lawyers Who Feel They Can't Take Vacations*' [findlaw.com], or '*Lawyers Need Vacations. Case Closed* [news.bloomberglaw.com], which starts with the sentence, "Lawyers often skip vacations, or work while away. . ."

Unfortunately, in the legal field, needing a break from work is often seen as an indication of weakness or the idea that the "sick" person can't keep up with the demands as compared to their peers. This is also connected to the expectation of the machine-like behavior we talked about earlier. And of course, a machine barely gets sick—if anything, it literally breaks or starts malfunctioning. Lawyers are not expected to need breaks, because the professional standard is that they are fully available and ready for the clients, *always.*

This standard only worsens in the private sector because of the famous billable hour. Though there's a movement within the legal profession trying to eradicate it—given the serious detriment it creates in lawyers' sense of worth and satisfaction—the expectation to work 24/7 is still there. In "An Open Letter to the Legal Profession,"[100] Jana Cohen Barbe, a Partner at Dentons, starts by saying:

> Dear Friends and Colleagues,
>
> The consensus is that there is a mental health crisis in the legal profession. That is no doubt true. High-profile suicides, admissions of substance abuse and addiction, and wholesale exits from the profession plague and torture all of us who still hold onto the view that ours is a noble and worthwhile vocation. . .

She moves on to explain how the billing system further reinforces unreasonable expectations in a lawyer's life:

> And yet, day-in and day-out, we record our time and know that our value as professionals is keyed, at least in part, to annual billable hours. The pressure then—to work seven days a week, to miss family events, to forgo vacations, to miss needed doctor's appointments—cannot be overstated. If you are like me, you feel guilty taking a Saturday or Sunday

100 Jana Cohen Barbe, *An Open Letter to the Legal Profession*, Thrive Global (Oct. 1, 2019), https://community.thriveglobal.com/open-letter-legal-profession/.

off, and it takes several days to let go of the guilt and begin to feel the relaxing effects of a vacation.

As Jana proposes, "[w]hat would happen if we fostered a culture where vacations were mandatory and professionals were instructed not to check email while out of the office?" But more importantly, **"[w]hy do law firms cling to a business model that we have known for decades is both antiquated and destructive?"**

I don't have the exact answer to those questions, but there are many incredible beings out there working on redesigning the business model behind law firms. As for now, however, bigger law firms continue to have a target of around 1,800 hours for partners and 2,200 hours for associates every year. This means the "24/7 available, no getting sick, no time off" lawyer identity is still very much alive—because otherwise that hourly target would be *impossible*[101] to reach.

The "adversarial & win-the-argument-at-all-costs" lawyer

A LAWYER SOMEWHERE: *Sir, you forgot to put ketchup on my burger and that was part of your bargain when I purchased this meal. I am gonna have to sue you.*

101 Here, we're talking 10-hour days, because you don't bill every hour from 8:00 am until 6:00 pm or all the time you spend at the office. There are several things you can't bill, including going the bathroom, talking to a colleague, your lunch time, a coffee break, etc. We're also talking, several—if not many, many weekends—during the year. If you're a law student and are curious about how the billable hour truly works, here's a recommended reading: Yale Law School Career Development Office, *The Truth About the Billable Hour*, https://law.yale.edu/sites/default/files/area/department/cdo/document/billable_hour.pdf. It's a very straightforward and honest description of how your year (and life) can look if you have this type of billing target at your law firm.

I haven't exactly said that in my life and I don't really dig burgers, but I promise you, I've fought about things in my daily life that I now realize I could have just let go of—except for the fact that I have been trained to be a lawyer so sometimes, I felt this need to win whatever the discussion was. And it is a bit embarrassing, or even one of my internal contradictions given that I also try to be a peaceful *yogi* in my life. That said, I like to see this not as a contradiction, but rather as a beautiful integration.

And of course, you might not have an aggressive lawyer inside of you, but please bear with me. Generally speaking, lawyers are often seen as being combative and competitive—and this is a generalization, but even if some do not enter law school with this combative nature, the educational system will make sure they develop that trait.

The American judicial system—as well as many other systems around the globe—is based on the premise that equitable solutions will emerge from the clash of *opposing* interests. This opposition necessarily creates conflict, and though mediation and more peaceful conflict resolution is starting to emerge as a countermovement, law schools still teaches law students to be combative and adversarial from day #1:

> *"You're the prosecutor in this case. Your job is to prove that you're right and that the defense is wrong. . ."*

This is a typical first-year legal analysis assignment—maybe not with those exact words, but that is the bottom line. There's nothing wrong with teaching law students how to advocate for their clients or how to analytically win a case. In fact, that is a necessary lawyer trait. The problem appears when the student interiorizes that "zealous" personality, erroneously thinking that an *aggressive* advocate is the equivalent of a successful lawyer. Or when the law student—and lawyer—cannot turn off this interiorized *aggressiveness* both in his life and interactions with others (e.g., colleagues, family, and friends).

We are trained to "fight zealously" for our clients because they deserve the best representation they can get—of course. However, if our system overemphasizes (and normalizes) this "zealous, angry, and winning-at-all-costs" lawyer trait, it will be very hard to turn it off once we get home. Once we internalize a belief system and reinforce it daily, it will become our way of thinking, neurologically speaking. It becomes how we think and see the world around us. Thus, if a conflict arises, we'll be inclined to become hostile and get very defensive because that is *what* we were taught in law school. That is how we were trained to *approach* that conflict. "*We must win and the other side is always trying to trick us*" becomes our way of thinking—even if the other side is literally our romantic partner.

In order for us to be able to relegate that combative mindset to the workplace, and utilize a more compassionate or neutral mindset with ourselves and with our loved ones, we first need the self-awareness to identify when we're operating in that mindset; and once we do that, we need the self-management to pause and prevent our autopilot from taking action based on the combative mindset and choose something more beneficial, peaceful, or less stress-inducing in the long term. Having the emotional intelligence skills to do that is not easy at all—it requires so much practice; and if I am really hungry and I've been waiting for my food for way too long, chances are I will fail the test. ^-*

The point is: self-awareness and self-management are both elements of emotional intelligence that law students are not taught, so for many, aggressiveness, hostility and a sense of feeling defensive starts driving their lives. On top of that, multiply all of the other thousands of lawyers who feel the same way and in turn attack their opponents. We might end with a playground of pretty aggressive kids.

There's this story about a man who was going to visit a friend for dinner. He hadn't seen his friend in a very long time. On the way to his friend's house, the man started fantasizing about whether his friend might have a cat (the man was allergic to cats). As he walked towards his friend's house, he could not stop thinking about it: *What if he has a cat? No way I am coming in. I mean, I could get really sick. He probably has a cat. Actually, he looks like a person who will have a cat. Why hasn't he told me? He should remember I am allergic to cats. That would be so inconsiderate of him… If he has a cat I am going to be so angry—I have so much work to do and I can't afford to get sick. He better not have a freaking cat... Gosh, why hasn't he said anything? This is bullshit…He better not have a damn cat!*

Throughout the whole walk, the man—who may or may not have been a lawyer because almost everybody engages in catastrophic thinking—thought of all the possible, negative hypothetical scenarios that could take place once he arrived at his friend's house. After the man knocked on the door, his friend excitedly opened it, and the man yelled:

THE MAN: *Dude, I am not going in! Why didn't you tell me you have a cat!?!?*

THE FRIEND: *Mmm, Hello to you too...? What are you talking about? I don't have a cat...Jeez, why are you so upset?*

Our minds are tricky. Negative hypothetical thinking is tricky. Reacting based on that thinking is tricky. And being defensive for no reason can for sure have an impact on our relationships. People get tired of us lawyers feeling attacked or having to win an incredibly low-stake, silly argument. Feeling like we have to "win" all the arguments is also really freaking tiring for our minds. Because the reality is that life on Earth shouldn't be a combative playfield. See what I am getting at?

When we don't know how to turn off this newly acquired "lawyer aggressiveness" skill in our interactions with others (e.g., family, friends, strangers...), we can develop a little of what's called phobic ideation. Phobic ideation involves an excessive preoccupation with a subject, situation or activity that triggers the phobia. In our context, it also means feeling disproportionately hostile and defensive towards others when a conflict arises. And because we haven't been taught how to have difficult conversations or deal with conflicts in more healthy ways, we directly jump onto the other's neck – like *a Rambo litigator*. We must therefore ask, is this practical? Is it healthy?

Another interesting dilemma also takes place when we're asked to defend a client whose cause we cannot come to terms with, even if we try very hard. The problem is that in law school, there is no space for that dilemma. We simply learn to ignore it, instead of mindfully moving through the emotional dissonance. As such, that self-dismissive behavior is the one we continue to reinforce once we enter the profession. Law school generally requires law students to "separate their morals from their professional identity as a lawyer."[102] In fact, as two authors put it,

> The Law school's curriculum is designed to neutralize that passion by imposing a rigor of thought that *divorces* law students from their feelings and morality.[103]

Let's imagine we're in the shoes of a law student or a young associate who went to law school to become an environmental or social justice activist. In class, during a discussion, or at work, that individual is *expected* to be highly motivated in defending the client's cause—whether it's a company that pollutes water and contaminates the entire population's food supply, or an insurance company that does not want to pay the medical bills of the plaintiff, who just lost her two parents in a car accident.

In this type of situation, a psychologist will tell you that it is pretty normal to start experiencing some sort of an identity crisis, or at least some difficulty reconciling two opposing realities. But instead of recognizing this and being willing to work through it, the traditional law school system unfortunately teaches students to always subordinate their moral values, empathies, and feelings about the case for the sake of victory—or even for the sake of a class discussion.

I recently had a one-on-one coaching client who was a first-year at Harvard Law School. One day, she was highly distressed because in one of her classes, a law professor had entertained a student's racist

102 Lauren Carasik, *Renaissance or Retrenchment: Legal Education at a Crossroads*, 44 Ind. L. Rev. 735, 750 (2011).

103 Jane Aiken & Stephen Wizner, *Law as Social Work*, 11 Wash. U. J.L. & Pol'y 63, 73 (2003) (emphasis added).

argument for the sake of the discussion. And while a lawyer must always come up with arguments for both sides, we have to ask whether taking humanity out of our legal analysis—or decisions—is truly contributing to the society we live in. And who knows, that student making the racist arguments might get to the Supreme Court one day, and his argument will be "legal" enough to change the course of history. Food for thought when we leave humanity out of the legal educational equation…

But back to our main question: what happens to that student or lawyer who is constantly having a moral clash? *Well, leave your job then*—some might say. And well, burning it all down is so much easier than integrating our contradictions. More importantly, not everybody has the privilege to decline a job offer or leave a job if they have a loan to pay. While an optimal amount of anger or aggressiveness might be very useful when facing a difficult case, it runs the risk of creating too much hostility, phobic ideation, or even the first signs of depression if we don't regulate it. A client expects a lawyer who will passionately defend his rights and cause, and who will fight opposing counsel accordingly. That is a very honorable skill to have as a lawyer, but we need to be able to regulate it so that it doesn't contaminate our emotional health and lives.

In their longitudinal study *Lawyer Distress*,[104] Beck, Sales, and Benjamin noted how anger was the strongest predictor of all the disorders found in lawyers, including anxiety, obsessive compulsiveness, interpersonal sensitivity, hostility, phobic ideation, and depression. And of course, that is just the tip of the iceberg because, as they

104 Beck et al., *supra* note 68, at 57.

warned us, "an alarming connection, described in the literature, is that alcohol releases anger and aggression."[105]

In fact, they found that anger is one of the strongest predictors of lawyers' mental health struggles. We are just starting to learn how to emotionally process the moral clash and discomfort when confronted by these moral dilemmas. But until we integrate this emotional skill, what do we do? We tend to numb[106]ourselves—whether we do it using alcohol, drugs, or burying the feelings with more work. Or maybe we start self-flagellating, telling ourselves, "*I am not cut out to be a lawyer*," or perhaps we procrastinate the job we need to get done (i.e., the source of our pain) and then get in trouble afterwards. Whatever the route, we don't know any better because we haven't been taught any better.

As for now, there is enough data to contraindicate the overemphasis (and glorification) of a "zealous and win-at-all-costs lawyer" *when* that emphasis is *not* accompanied by the skill to regulate it, so that it doesn't translate into feelings of anger, hostility, and even depression. Does this exaggerated trait serve our profession in the long-term?

---

105 *Id.* at 53.

106 Emotional numbing is defined as the process of shutting out our feelings so that we do not feel or express our emotions. It's also a common coping mechanism if we have experienced trauma or are experiencing really strong, difficult emotions. While it might be useful as a short-term escape at times, numbing is not sustainable as a long-term solution because what we don't process, will stay stuck in the body (which we may later somatize). Somatization is the process by which a person experiences psychological or emotional distress as physical symptoms, without an identifiable medical or physical cause. In other words, somatizing is the conversion of emotional or psychological distress into physical symptoms.

Other covert [but equally damaging] narratives

Apart from these obvious lawyer traits or identities, there are also other hidden narratives that continue to covertly operate in the profession. For example, Professor Young speaks of something we don't openly talk about either:

> At multiple [law] schools, LGBTQIA+ students have told me that the career services staff advises them to dress in gender-conforming ways—for example, telling butch lesbians who feel comfortable in a men's suit to dress in a women's suit or telling a gender nonbinary person to dress in a way that conforms to their assigned sex at birth. On a superficial level, this advice 'makes sense,' because employers sometimes discriminate against people who appear queer. But it also gives students the very clear message that the legal profession does not welcome who they are.[107]

Additionally, Young notes how this systematic behavior in law schools "puts the responsibility for change on the shoulders of the people who are disadvantaged by the system." Young also acknowledges that "questions like this are not easy to answer, but we have to understand how destructive it is simply to tell students to 'try to look normal so employers will hire you' and leave it at that."

But no, an institution that charges almost 200k to law students cannot afford to just '*leave it that.*' There needs to be a responsibility or at least a sense of deep care for how the educational system

107 Young, *supra* note 45, at n. 75.

is impacting the psychological health of students. And, thankfully, there are incredible people[108] within certain law schools who are fighting to make a healthier, more compassionate law school into a reality.

As for my personal experience, I remember when I started my first job as a foreign trainee at a mid-size law firm in Detroit. One of my mentors was a very kind old man who had argued a case before the Supreme Court. He had also been the CEO of the firm. He taught me a million things and I'm forever grateful for his wisdom. But interestingly, he once told me: *don't put too many activist positions on your resume. That tells the employer you might be a troublemaker.* Bill, who had a grandiose heart, just wanted to help me and make sure I got hired—just as Career Services advisors at a law school do when they counsel students. But the underlying issue is that the submissive, close to slave-like, gender-conforming, and other harmful stereotypes that continue to be enforced within the legal field are not a healthy road to progress—quite the opposite.

Finally, and to say goodbye to this chapter, I want you to imagine the life of a third-year law student with me. This student is already internalizing the stereotypical identities we just covered. He is also struggling with anxiety, or is already experiencing the first signs of depression while still in law school. Given his state of mind, he is starting to consider whether it is a good idea to disclose his mental health state so that he can get the help he needs. However, the fear—of not being admitted to the bar, the potential loss of credibility among his peers, or the loss of social status as the *Type A, perfect*

108 Though I wasn't able to cite every author or administrator who advanced the issue of law students' and lawyers' mental health, I wanted to say thank you to every single person who has.

student who now *admits to be struggling* with mental health—simply overtakes him. On a physiological level, his muscles start tensing day after day, and the obsessive thoughts about what to do, and what happens if somebody finds out, continue. What will this student do?

For the sake of applying an objective view, let's use the cost-benefit analysis from torts. For starters, it might seem like this student has a lot to lose if he discloses his pain—i.e., potential loss of bar admission, job prospects, credibility among peers, translated into a loss of networking opportunities and so on. The benefits could be improved health. However, in the short term, the potential loss could be bigger—especially after the huge financial, emotional, and logistical investment this student has made to attend law school and become a lawyer. Moreover, disclosing his mental health could corroborate an internal, or collective, belief that he has not met the standard of perfection his other peers are indeed meeting (at least on the outside). Of course, barely anyone around him talks openly about mental health, so he will probably feel completely alone in his pain (though in reality, there are so many people struggling, just like him). Unfortunately, his law school doesn't really address mental health either.

What do you think will happen to this student? Will he be supported and take assertive action on his mental health, or will he likely suffer in silence?

6

The Legal Mind:

a new way of thinking and seeing the world

[W]hen one develops a habitual way of looking for patterns, whether it is the way in which falling blocks fit together or a particular way of analyzing logical problems (thinking like a lawyer), the brain builds neuro-pathways that tend to channel one's thinking through the same pathway, even when one is not engaging in the activity that initially created the neuro-pathway.

— Todd David Peterson, *The Moral Obligation of Law Schools to Address Law Student Well-being: A Review Essay About The Happy Lawyer*, 30 NOTRE DAM J.L. ETHICS & PUB POL'Y 67, 75 (2016).

In this chapter, we'll dissect the specific ways our *legal* mind is trained to think, as well as the implications of repetitive negative thinking. As lawyers, we are mainly taught to think in five ways:

1. Identify who is at fault in a given situation (i.e., **fault-finding thinking**).
2. Identify all errors or mistakes for both sides (i.e., **error-finding thinking**).
3. Identify all potential pitfalls, risks, or negative scenarios that may arise in a given case (i.e., **hypothetical negative thinking**).
4. Anticipate what the other side's conduct and attack will be (i.e., **defensive/adversarial thinking**).
5. Compete and work really hard, because competitiveness reigns inside of law school and in legal practice (i.e., **highly competitive thinking**).

A *legal mind* should have internalized these five ways of thinking before they enter the profession, and the majority of law schools put a tremendous emphasis on students acquiring this type of thinking during their legal training.

Fault-finding thinking

Who's at fault here?

This question is the cornerstone of law school education and the basis for our adversarial legal system. Law Professor Todd Peterson did a beautiful job explaining how this "fault-finding" thinking affects the law student's mind and psyche. When we consistently train our mind to look at things in a particular way (i.e., like a lawyer), we will start looking at the world in this fashion, even after we have left law school or gone home from the law firm office. He referred to this as a Tetris effect that happens in law school. As Peterson perfectly articulates it:

> Law school is a three-year lesson in pessimism. It begins in the first year as students are trained both subconsciously and consciously to anticipate bad outcomes and problems in the future. The torts class is a semester-long exposure to all the bad things that can happen in life. There is no better illustration of the Tetris effect than the too-familiar stories of law students going home for Christmas and seeing everything around them as a source of potential negligence actions.[109]

The more we train our minds to look at things in a particular way, the more we'll start seeing things in *that* particular way. The concept of neuroplasticity is illustrative here. Broadly defined, neuroplasticity is the ever-changing ability of the brain to create synapses (i.e., connections) between cells; these connections become stronger or weaker depending on the flow of information between them. As such, repetitive experience—such as a repetitive way of thinking—has the power to create new connections in our brain, and therefore modify it.

---

109 Todd David Peterson, *The Moral Obligation of Law Schools to Address Law Student Well-being: A Review Essay About The Happy Lawyer*, 30 ND J. L. Ethics & Pub Pol'y 67, 75-76 (2016).

Think of our brains as a power grid filled with connected pathways that are activated every time we think, move, or feel. The more these pathways are used, the stronger they get. Thus, if we consistently—and repetitively—enforce fault-finding as a way of thinking, such as what happens in the mind of a law student or a lawyer, we will ultimately strengthen the connections in our brain dealing with that type of thinking, thereby reinforcing it.[110]

Lawyers assign fault in legal cases. That's what we are trained to do. And this is not a bad thing—it's a skill, especially if you're trying to assign fault in a medical malpractice claim, for example. The problem arises when that way of thinking transcends the professional arena and spills into our personal lives. When we are trained to assign fault, we interiorize the premise that there's always someone or something to blame. We start seeing conflicts with other humans as combat, where we need to assign fault to one of the parties involved; but aren't human relationships much more complicated than that?

In life, there are unpredictable situations where there is no one or nothing to blame—things happen and even if we try to find a cause or a guilty party, there are times when we won't find anything. We've all experienced this. Thus, while many legal problems can be approached through a fault-finding fashion, we need a different, more peaceful way to approach life. And if life hasn't taught us that truth already, it will.

---

110 Conversely, this neuroplasticity also gives us the opportunity to rewire our brains and shift the way we think or feel to more positive, nurturing ways—we'll talk more about this in Part III.

Error-finding thinking

What's wrong, mistaken, missing, or simply 'not perfect' here?

When I am working on an immigration appeal, the first thing I do is read the Immigration Judge's decision. I first identify the reasons for the denial, then I analyze if those reasons are substantiated by the record, and as I'm doing all of this, I'm looking for errors. That is, errors, mistakes, or omissions on the Immigration Judge's part. *Did he not analyze this issue properly? Did he forget to take X into consideration?* Etcetera.

While every area of the law has its own intricacies, a case generally involves opposing parties. Whether we're trying to settle and negotiate, or submit motions in court, we're looking for leverage. We're looking for the errors, the mistakes, the weak points so that we can win the case or settle in a way that works for us. Again, that's what we do, and often beautifully so. But when unchecked, and spilled into our personal lives, this type of thinking has two important implications:

- If we're so used to looking for errors in another lawyer's brief, decision, or case; we will, more likely than not, be equally *harsh* towards our own professional or personal projects. We will become overly self-judgmental towards our performance because we know there are other lawyers out there who will also scrutinize every instance of our work—and we know this first hand.

- Because there's 'somebody watching' or 'waiting for us to make a mistake,' we become *overly perfectionistic* in a very legitimate attempt to protect ourselves from the other side's attack. Therefore, we establish a *standard of perfection as our survival mechanism*. And we will, without a doubt, procrastinate a project unless it is close to perfection, because we're terrified we will be judged. As lawyers, we know we will be on the spot[111] for our mistakes (even though it is human to make those).

Negative hypothetical thinking

What can go wrong here?
List all potential scenarios so we cover all of our bases.

To become a competent attorney, the law student must learn how to anticipate any potential problems with her client's case. We must (and are trained to) protect our client's interests; therefore, we must be able to sort-of-predict the future and every worst-case scenario that could affect our client. In doing so, we must think of the worst-case scenarios because that is the only way we will cover all angles of the situation. That is how we will be *ready*. As such, we must always pose the question of: what can go wrong? And when I say "what," I mean this: "Let's analyze every possible negative scenario that can take place."

---

111 During a cold call, a federal clerkship interview with a hypercompetitive clerk who is asking you to recite some amendment, a hearing, a meeting with a certain partner…

This type of hypothetical thinking involves imagining [negative] possibilities and consequences that have not yet taken place. Catastrophic thinking can include ruminating about irrational, worst-case scenarios—which of course creates anxiety in the thinker and can later evolve into more serious disorders when done repetitively.[112] As Professor Peterson emphasized,

> The pessimism training continues in a more conscious way in other classes, where students are taught to anticipate potential problems and plan for them in advance. Students trained to anticipate problems in their roles as lawyers will inevitably anticipate problems and approach life more pessimistically even when they leave the school building.[113]

Let me give you a couple of examples:

- So, 'I'm in love and I'm thinking about getting married' *(lists all potential relationship problems that may arise in the future*).
- 'My romantic partner hasn't arrived yet, maybe something bad has happened' (*lists potential disasters*).

---

112 *See e.g.*, Resham Gellatly et al., *Catastrophic Thinking: A Transdiagnostic Process Across Psychiatric Disorders*, 40 Cognitive Therapy & Research 441, 441-452 (2016) (noting the association between catastrophic thinking and psychological disorders).

113 Peterson, *supra* note 109, at 75-76.

- 'The law firm partner hasn't replied to my email' (*lists all possible mistakes or omissions*—though the partner was just busy playing golf).

- 'We're not billing as much this month' (*lists and unconsciously chooses to believe the worst-case scenarios for the firm, even though billing has fluctuated in the past and things have gone well*).

- 'My performance hasn't been stellar this year; I will get fired.' (*visualizes himself as a homeless person, among many other catastrophic scenarios*).

Anyway, pick your poison.

Defensive & adversarial thinking

In addition to protecting our clients in other parallel realities and hypothetical scenarios, we internalize another premise:

The other side might attack or trick us.

It's a fight, this is not *la la-land.* Can we even imagine a lawyer without the illusion of combat in the picture? And the fact that we are warriors who can fight against our opponents is not necessarily a bad thing. Again, it's a lawyer skill. The problem is when this combative readiness becomes pathological, when we take it to the extreme and internalize it as a general mode of operating, or when we have to constantly defend ourselves because we believe that everybody is always trying to trick us—some way, somehow. Apart from that being exhausting in itself, it's a very straightforward recipe for unhappiness.

When law students and lawyers use this way of thinking every day of the week for at least ten hours a day (and let's add weekends for many), we are solidifying this type of thinking in our brain. And by repetition, we can't help but to spill it over onto our partner, the coffee barista, or the cashier. And yes, there are nasty people out there that require a more aggressive response, but what happens when we use this type of thinking in our daily interactions with other humans we love and care about? With ourselves?

Neuroscientist Patrick Cavanagh explains that our brains bend our perception of reality to meet our desires or expectations, which is why we end up seeing and experiencing the given story or narrative that we've created for ourselves.[114] How many times have you felt attacked when you weren't?

Simply put, if we are trained to think that the other side—or the world—is going to trick us, we will likely feel defensive and we will perceive hostility. If we deal with conflict—and life—as if it were a constant combat situation, finding faults right and left, our ability to deal with and resolve conflict might be a little aggressive, don't you think? If we walk around seeing the world as a battlefield and as a space filled with potential negative scenarios, maybe we won't be the most optimistic and positive people in the room (I guess the

114 Vox (Brian Resnick), *"Reality" is Constructed by your Brain. Here Is What that Means, and Why it Matters,* Wu Tsai Neuroscience Institute · Stanford University (June 22, 2020), www.neuroscience.stanford.edu.

TV stereotype that lawyers are aggressive or unhappy starts to make more sense now…)

Highly competitive thinking

Who's better?

America is the mecca of competition. I'm not going to criticize that because I like competing—and when done with a team, it can be a pretty amazing thing. The problem? As always, the extremes. We've seen why law school is one of the most competitive educational institutions. There's an obsession with performance because we internalize the fact that our value—and survival—rests on the external: grades, accomplishments, titles, awards, and so on. This obsession is rooted in the need and expectation to compete. Hence why the long hours, days, weeks, or months without a break are justified and normalized. *That's what it takes to be a successful lawyer*, one may argue. I mean, yes—hard work is required to become successful at anything; but I don't think hard work and mental wellbeing are mutually exclusive. Sacrificing one for the other should not be the solution, either.

We must try to find balance. And it's easy for me to write those words, but I strive for it every day of my life. Sometimes I attain it and other times I don't, but I keep practicing. In law school, and in the legal profession, excessive workload demands are normalized. Interiorized as the standard to embrace and follow. We also learn that we need to be winners, the best, or better *than* X. Why? Because that's our measuring instrument; that's how we learned to filter people before, during, and after law school. And can you blame us? We *compete* for the grades—and for the jobs that will pay our debts. And just as we compete against our classmates in law school, we compete against our colleagues within the firm (even if we do it silently).

From an organizational standpoint, excessive competitiveness creates a hostile and uncomfortable environment. On an individual level, it is a recipe for frustration and dissatisfaction. We cannot be *the* best all the time. There will always be someone who will outperform us, or do something that we haven't done. When we compare ourselves with others, we rarely take into account the other person's personal life experiences. What's worse is that there's no real race to win—there's just endless, infinite competition because there will always be more to accomplish. And so we're stuck in an endless cycle.

Psychological implications of repetitive negative thinking

Finally, when we consistently operate with our legal mind running the show, we risk making it our default, autopilot mode. And while legal thinking is an obvious component of being a lawyer, not knowing how to offset its downside effects can be detrimental to both our mental and physical health.[115]

---

115 Research shows that repetitive negative thinking—such as imagining worst case scenarios, constantly identifying errors in ourselves and others, or thinking that the world is out to get us—constitutes a risk factor for anxiety and depression. *See e.g.,* Mina Stefanovic et al., *Is a High Association Between Repetitive Negative Thinking and Negative Affect Predictive of Depressive Symptoms? A Clustering Approach for Experience-Sampling Data,* 10.1 Clinical Psychological Science, *10*(1), 74–89 (2021) (noting, among others, the reciprocal relationship between repetitive negative thinking and negative affect); Ehring T. et al., *Repetitive Negative Thinking as a Transdiagnostic Process,* 1.3 Int' J. Cognitive Therapy 192-205 (2008) (emphasizing that high

In multiple ways, overstimulation of the legal mind can interfere with our experience of life. If we're trained to obsessively imagine all worst-case scenarios, we'll feel anxious as we do that in our personal life. If we think that other people are out to get us (just like opposing counsel), we'll just exist in a state of perceived hostility and defensiveness for no reason. If we're compulsively trying to compete or prove our worth, we might be upset more often than not, because we can't be the best all the time. When the prospect of doing something new appears, we might feel frozen, because what if we make a mistake or end up being 'bad at it'? We might feel terrified at the idea of submitting an article for publication because 'what if the topic isn't interesting enough' or 'what if somebody else has written about it and my contribution will be useless'? We might end up not submitting the piece, or not applying for the job, the workshop, the hobby, or the thing we wanted—mainly out of fear.

Unfortunately, negative thoughts tend to play on repeat, and we create endless storylines and hypothetical scenarios about them, a Hollywood production in our heads. Apart from wasting our precious time, it hurts. And let me be clear: the lawyer's mind is a beautiful thing. It's brilliant. It allows us to fight, advocate, and creatively argue a case. We need it for the type of work we do. But we need to find ways to offset its impact outside of our work. When we adopt our lawyer thinking as our default or autopilot thinking, we will suffer more. And maybe that's one of the reasons why lawyers are three times more likely to suffer from depression than any other professionals. If we become masters at anticipating (or creating)

levels of repetitive negative thinking are present across a large range of disorders and appear to be causally involved in the maintenance of emotional problems).

negative hypothetical scenarios for the sake of our client's protection, we need to develop self-awareness and the proper reframing tools to prevent this type of negative thinking from contaminating the rest of our lives; as well as to protect ourselves. And that's where we're headed on the next part of this book.

Part iii

•

Becoming an emotionally intelligent lawyer

*

Considering that many law students will one day hold crucial positions in our communities, we need to reflect on what type of lawyers our communities truly need. In previous chapters, we've seen how outdated our current legal educational system can be, and how we ought to redefine the lawyer identity in order to safeguard the mental health of law students and lawyers.

The thing is, if we don't have legislators, justices and lawyers who have developed empathy—a basic pillar of emotional intelligence (and humanity)—we risk creating a world where uncompassionate laws will be written and inhumane legal decisions will be dictated, thereby stripping peoples' rights and damaging the earth and our communities.

Moreover, we tend to only look at the symptoms, rather than addressing the actual cause and root of the problem. In fact, one of the reasons why, as humans, we keep repeating the same behaviors and mistakes is that we don't address the root of the problem we're facing. Merely focusing on the symptom is a short-term strategy, and we need long-term healing. As humans, if someone or something bothers us, we try to eliminate them—we don't investigate what in them triggers us or what childhood wound they opened. If we have anxiety, we take medication. We don't generally undergo a longer therapy process (that's harder, or incredibly expensive, or we simply don't have time for it). If we don't like something about us or our body, we try to eradicate it as well—we don't attempt to accept it and love ourselves just as we are (because that's the hardest thing to do). So, as a short-term solution, we choose the easy, fast path because the longer one requires us to look at the things that we don't like about ourselves. And that's way too painful.

In the legal profession, we do the same. We do not want to look deep, deep down. As members of a respectable, honorable and elitist profession, we seek refuge in the illusion of perfection, monetary success, and status we've created. I mean, *we're smart; because not everyone has what it takes to become—and be—a lawyer, right?* The truth, however, is that, as a profession, we are pretty depressed and anxious. We're overthinking everything way too much. We're a little more obsessive than the average. We're fighting when we might not want to. And deep down, we're suffering—even if we don't want to accept it because we think that accepting that fact makes us weak. And yes, many are making a hell of a lot of money, but also drinking too much and taking Prozac or other substances that numb us. Additionally, many of us have already attempted to leave the traditional form of the profession because we are unhappy.

So there's that—and we need to look into all of it, as painful as it might be. Our profession deserves to heal. Our law students deserve to feel supported. Our lawyers deserve to be healthy. And if you're not a lawyer, chances are your life will be impacted by a lawyer or two, one day— a friend, a partner, a judge, a law professor, a government legislator, a politician. In our world, things are more interconnected than we think. So, the question now becomes,

How do we bring healing to the legal profession?

There are many answers and angles to this question. I'll give you what I came here to give you; in no way do I proclaim myself the owner of answers or truth. Rather, my approach is simply the product of my work, life experience and investigation of the matter.

I rest in knowing that future generations will come, and therefore question it, deconstruct it, make it better, and ultimately take what's useful and leave what's not.

The next two chapters deal with the ways we can start to bring positive change to our profession.

- First, we must redefine the lawyer identity and close the gap between detrimental stereotypes and the real human behind the lawyer title. In other words, we ought to humanize the profession and reframe structural narratives within it (*Chapter 7 · Redefining & Humanizing the Lawyer Identity*).

- Then, we've got to provide lawyers with the emotional intelligence skills necessary to navigate the stressors of the profession (*Chapter 8 · Emotional Intelligence for the Legal Mind*).

Finally—and to ensure that healing will engender long-term and lasting change—we need to integrate these skills early on and at the very root of every lawyer's journey: *law school.* Part IV will cover much needed reforms in law school teaching.

Ultimately, the bottom line to the reader is this: *problems are better solved at the root.* In other words, rather than focusing on adding mental health resources to law schools, we need to prevent law students from needing those in the first place. The same preventive logic applies to law firms, non-profits, and so on. Instead of dealing only with the symptoms and ignoring the real cause behind the problem, this book aims to crack us open, *for good.*

7

Redefining and Humanizing the Lawyer Identity

*

Lawyers feel, too.

The fact that lawyers feel was a realization I had when I was taking a class called *Professional Responsibility in the Public Interest* at Penn Law School, with Shannon Browning. It was 2015; I was 24 years old and, as a class assignment, had written a piece called "*The Need for Emotional Intelligence in the Legal Field.*" I am 32 years old now, and I continue to do my inner work on perfectionism, impostor's syndrome, alignment, self-compassion, and so on—all things that are present within my work, legal practice, and personal projects. Since little, I always felt I was "too sensitive," and when I started law school, I realized *feeling* didn't have that much space to exist.

As a multidisciplinary person, I try to find the balance between my practice as a solo, virtual immigration lawyer/appellate writer, as a coach and EI educator for law students and lawyers, and as a human being who values naps and her freedom[116]very freaking much. It ain't easy, but it's worth the try. One of the most interesting things I've learned through my work on coaching law students, delivering workshops, teaching them how to outline, write A+ exams, and so on, is this:

> There is a new generation of lawyers who want to have *balance*, *freedom*, and *emotional health* in their careers.

Yep, these emerging attorneys want to be well, feel what they need to feel, and do what they want to do. They quickly identify the slave-like grind. They see the flaws in the system. And while some don't have another option but to enter the game in order to pay off their loans, the majority of the students I've met are reluctant to put

116 I'm a Gemini sun and Sagittarius moon (hence my inner need to explore so many things); and a projector in Human Design (the naps!).

up with the merciless, hustle culture of the legal profession. They want something better for themselves. These students are mostly Gen-z; but my generation (millennials)—are becoming acutely aware of the same epiphanies. I can safely say that almost all of my intimate friends from law school have either left Biglaw, shifted careers, or are seriously thinking about it. And it is not because they didn't like the law. It was mainly because the legal field was destroying their mental and physical health. Some law firm partners in the back will be like: *Well, suck it up. These newer generations are so weak, always whining!*

Well, the truth is, the majority of millennials and Gen-z kindly (and privately) respond to this as: *With all due respect, your old way of thinking doesn't make any f*cking sense!*[117] Many are going solo, becoming virtual lawyers on IG, becoming online entrepreneurs, merging the law with other disciplines, creating their own version of a 'career'... Whatever its form, that silent rebellion is shunning the old lawyer system and its accompanying stereotypes. The reason? That old system is detrimental to our health.

Previous generations interiorized a lawyer persona who was highly trained to work and operate in the world as a perfect, unbreakable, rational machine. That same machine was trained to spot mistakes, anticipate negative hypothetical scenarios and assign faults to parties—without seemingly producing any damage inside of its internal system. Today, we know that there is a human being behind that machine. We also know that some of the functions the "machine" consistently operates on (i.e., 'thinking like a lawyer') can have a detrimental effect on its executive center (i.e., the region that deals with the "machine's" life) if we don't regulate them properly. We

117 Excuse my language, but I get passionate!

have the information, we are just scared of change. And yes, change is scary and uncertain; but also necessary for our survival and growth.

Closing the gap between the machine-lawyer and the human, emotional being

The first thing we need to do as a collective is to close the gap between the machine—which a lawyer is *expected to be*—and the human being a lawyer *truly is*. In other words, we need to humanize being a lawyer. As mentioned before, there has always been a gap between the popular lawyer's identity (i.e., as a perfect, non-emotional individual) and the identity within a lawyer's real life (i.e., an individual with real problems and human emotions). That gap starts in law school—specifically with an overemphasis on rationality and the subsequent "cabining" of our emotions. This is where the unreasonable expectation starts. How are we supposed to operate like a rock with no emotions when we have to argue for something we don't believe in, or something inhuman? Human rights violations? Racism? LGBTQIA+ Discrimination? Abortion? Rape? Pollution that kills?

We have feelings; we care, too. And yet, when we receive a case —regardless of whether it is against or aligned with our values— we're expected to not be affected or bothered by it, to any extent. If we don't believe in it, we are still expected to perfectly align with the cause and empathize with our client's goals.

Rule 1.2 says *"A lawyer must act with commitment and dedication to the interests of the client and with zeal in advocacy upon the client's behalf."* There is nothing wrong with passionate advocacy, but how does it affect the attorney's psyche if she or he does not know how to process a moral clash or emotional dissonance? How do we address the distress this inner conflict creates? What happens if the lawyer lacks the emotional skills to deal with and offset the dissonance or negative feelings that arise from it?

Take Miriam. She is a first-year Muslim associate who is expected to be highly motivated in defending a company that has a clear discriminatory policy towards Muslims, even though one of the reasons she went to law school was to address social justice in her community as well as defend freedom of speech and religion. Regardless of Miriam's potential inner conflict, she is expected to zealously advocate for the firm's client, a multimillion dollar business. And no, it's not like Miriam can say "no, I don't want to be involved"—that's the equivalent of professional suicide in most instances, and we know that.

For starters, this scenario will require Miriam to subordinate her own values, which can temporarily destabilize her moral grounding if she does not know how to detach from the case in a healthy way. Then there are various elements at play here. First, and as a lawyer, there is an expectation (coming from the firm and the profession itself) to remain perfectly rational despite the emotional dissonance she might be feeling inside. Based on this widely accepted expectation, she has no room or institutional approval to express her discomfort; or in other words, her emotional problem, though rooted in her legal practice, rests solely on her shoulders.

Second, most likely, Miriam has no coping skills to process this dissonance on her own. She didn't learn them in law school. For that, she would have needed training in self-awareness, self-compassion, and self-management in order to deal with the emotional complexity of her situation.[118] Third, if Miriam happens to be highly sensitive or an empath, she might be experiencing higher levels of stress, or empathic burnout,[119]without even knowing it. What would normally happen is that Miriam won't have time to deal with her internal problem. She has too much on her plate at work, and she barely has time for herself. Therefore, she will likely suffer in silence and unconsciously enforce a machine-based system that doesn't allow her to be a human experiencing an emotional dissonance.

With no institutional or community support to express her struggles, Miriam will also internalize that she should somewhat hide it or "not be bothered at all" by the emotional dissonance she's feeling. Similar to her 1L experience—where nobody opens up about mental health struggles—Miriam will unconsciously perpetuate the status quo in the legal field. After all, her mental health is not the priority for her firm —even though her performance is inextricably connected to the client's representation. How many Miriams are there in the legal world?

If we are expected to be empathic with our clients and zealously advocate for their cause—i.e., be somewhat emotionally attached—how are we also expected not to be empathic towards ourselves? This contradiction results in an unrealistic expectation that attorneys should have empathy when dealing with their clients, but that such empathy cannot affect them in *any* rational capacity. As mentioned, there is no such a thing as emotional, selective numbing. We can't just say, "*Oh, I don't wanna feel this. Let me eradicate it.*" Unfortunately,

118 Even though lawyers encounter emotionally complex cases all the time, emotional intelligence has never been seen as a top skill to acquire in law school.

119 Empathic burnout is a state of emotional exhaustion that stems from a person extending too much emotional, mental, and physical energy while caring for someone else.

no—it'd be nice sometimes, but no. If we numb the uncomfortable/painful emotions, we are, by default, also numbing joy, love, belonging and other emotions that give meaning to our lives.

With no emotional skills or ways to integrate the contradiction, many lawyers numb themselves in an attempt to survive and continue with the job. But such numbing is unhealthy in the long term, especially when we do it consistently, on a daily basis. I mean, what lawyer or law student hasn't faced this numbing/avoidance dilemma? *"I need to keep going. I can't let this emotion affect my case or my job."* Again, we are trying to survive in the legal world—and we do it the best we can, because nobody gave us the emotional tools. As such, if Miriam has no emotional skills to deal with the emotional dissonance she is feeling at work, she might numb herself continuously. One case after the other. Why? Because she needs to keep going. She needs to survive. Or she might collapse one day and leave. How will that behavior impact her life and mental health in the long term?

Neither you, I, or the legal field can't decide to eliminate emotions from the equation (it's impossible). We just need to learn how to regulate them effectively. As lawyers, we need to normalize the fact that we're human beings who suffer and feel—like everybody else. Our vulnerability is an intrinsic part of us; it is not some liability we need to get rid of (again, we can't). Only by accepting this simple truth can we start destigmatizing mental health struggles in our profession. Only by humanizing ourselves—and reclaiming our emotional nature—can we liberate ourselves from the stigma, thereby shifting the narrative that "lawyers who struggle with mental health are weak, undesirable or flawed."

If we look honestly at the larger statistics, one way or another, we *all* struggle with something. Anxiety, postpartum depression, obsessive thinking, stress, grief, and so on. Who doesn't need to go to therapy in the twenty-first century? We barely know how to process complex emotions (and what a true gift if you had the privilege to learn or can afford how to learn it now). We are not perfect machines at work. Lawyers are human beings who feel, struggle, suffer; therefore, in order to close the gap, we need to humanize that hidden truth—individually and collectively. And, after all, we are social beings built into an emotional fabric. That is how the human race has survived.

Creating a more inclusive, multifaceted lawyer stereotype

Apart from humanizing the profession and normalizing the fact that lawyers are emotional beings, we also need to make space for the lawyer who is not the Rambo litigator we've consistently seen on TV. What about the future scholars, law professors, researchers, policy makers, legislators, consultants, mediators, ambassadors, and more? There's nothing wrong with being the attractive and aggressive Harvey Specter from the show Suits.[120] In fact, we need people like that. But we can't make such aggression *a necessary* trait for everybody because there are people who have other traits that are equally effective. I'm talking about the conflict manager, the healer, the peacemaker. These legal professionals exist, too. There are law students who will never be involved in an adversarial, litigator-like scene once they graduate. And even though that is a statistical fact,

120 Sorry for the spoiler *-* but Harvey ends up having to go to (really expensive) therapy because he starts having panic attacks.

most law schools are solely designed to uphold, and are dedicated to, the aggressive litigator stereotype from the 19th century:

Competitive.

Cut-throat.

Unbreakable.

Not emotional.

Only rational.

Winning.

And only winning.

An illustration inspired from a scene on the TV show Suits

While there are law schools that offer a myriad of alternative courses dealing with mediation or other legal avenues, I am most concerned with the foundational training of the 1L curriculum. That's so because most Career Services departments barely offer 1L students anything different than the "law firm" path (of course, have in mind the *US News* & employability rankings). As a consequence, our legal training overemphasizes the TV stereotype in the illustration above.

To redefine that figure and make it more inclusive, we need to expand the lawyer identity to include different types of personalities within the spectrum. From the aggressive litigator to the peaceful healer, we need to offer law students alternative ways to put their legal training to use; or, at a minimum, the opportunity to explore who they want to be (we'll cover that in chapter 8).

One thing is certain. If we want a generation of lawyers who are not numbing themselves or self-medicating to deal with the pressure or the stereotypes they don't feel aligned with, we need emotionally intelligent lawyers who are able to *regulate their emotions* and who know *who they are* at their core. With this, we're onto chapter 8—let's go. *-*

8

Emotional Intelligence for the Legal Mind

Before you start reading, please grab a notebook or a piece of paper and a pen. This is going to be an interactive chapter. I'd love for you to take your time with it—**and know that you'll be tempted to just read it and skip the exercises, but I caution you not to** [*been there, done that*]. Transformation and understanding require us to go from the theoretical to actual application. Just as a brief would be nothing without the application of the rules in it, the same logic applies here. I am also attaching a TikTok screenshot of my cat Niva supervising my journaling work, with the ulterior motive to convince you to actively engage with this chapter:

Meow reader, thank you for doing this work with me. — Niva

A very brief introduction before we dive into emotional intelligence-based exercises:

In 1990, Peter Salovey and John Mayer defined emotional intelligence as "the ability to monitor one's own and other people's emotions, to discriminate among them, and use this information to guide thinking and behavior." I see emotional intelligence as the ability to interact with yourself and the world in a positive and productive way. I also see it as a way *not* to cause yourself or others needless suffering. While I was growing up, emotional intelligence wasn't important, or at least it wasn't considered a "skill;" but those days are over and emotional intelligence is now recognized as *the* ultimate skill to navigate this human experience we call *life*.

In chapter 6, we learned how the legal mind works. This chapter will teach us ways to offset the negative consequences of constantly operating through the lens of that legal mind—that is, fault-finding, error-finding, hypothetical negative or catastrophic, defensive and adversarial, or highly competitive thinking. Or, in other words, pessimistic and rigid thinking. Since law schools are still in the process of implementing institutional interventions to address law students' (and lawyers') mental health crises, let this chapter serve as an alternative, so that we can start integrating positive change on an individual level, right now. The ideal scenario is to journey with a therapist, a coach, a trusted friend or someone who provides a safe space for you. If none of those are available, it's okay. There's still much to gain from doing these exercises.

We're going to cover the following areas:

- **Self-awareness:** identifying recurring & self-sabotaging narratives.
- **Reframing:** reinterpreting those narratives using a growth mindset & self-compassion.
- **Grounding:** mindfulness and presence for the overthinking mind.
- **Boundaries:** saying no & managing energy leaks.
- **Alignment:** discovering what *truly* matters to you.

Finally, the structure is going to be as follows:

1) I'll define the theoretical concept [*Definition*]; and

2) Then give you a "Do it Yourself"[121] (DIY) exercise so you can apply that concept to your own, unique, real life [*Self-reflective DIY exercise*].

The thing is, I'm not gonna tell you to sit and meditate if you prefer to do shaking or ecstatic dance in order to connect to your body. What I'll do, instead, is guide you and give you tools to explore, personalize, and build your own emotional skill-set. In the end, *you are your own guru*, so what worked for me doesn't necessarily need to to work for you. Apply that same logic when you read other books or see other coaches. Take what resonates and leave what doesn't. Keep gathering information, and *do you, at all times.*

---

121 While this chapter has obvious limitations (e.g., it's not a substitute for therapy), it still allows you to start a healing journey on your own. It can make you think about things you haven't had the time, the support, or the motivation to think about. So I encourage you to try and see how it feels.

Okay, grab the pen (and paper) if you haven't, pleazzze ^-^ We're starting!

. . .

Self-awareness: identifying recurring and self-sabotaging narratives

*

What is your recurring self-talk?

1) The first thing we need to do is become aware of the way we talk to ourselves. Our self-talk is a mirror into how we interpret the events that happen to us and the stories/conclusions we create around them. *"She didn't say anything...that probably means she didn't like my piece." "I am probably looking like an idiot; I am terrible at this." "Everybody else seems to be fine. There's probably something wrong with me."* These are some examples of self-sabotaging narratives.

As explained in previous chapters, most of us tend to be over-achievers and the legal mind is trained to operate as a highly competitive, perfectionistic, and negative hypothetical scenario-creator. This type of thinking will likely lead to higher doses of impostor's syndrome, harsh self-criticism, obsessive negative thinking, and/or empathic burnout. Becoming conscious and aware of these tendencies is the first step to protecting our mental health. But how do we become aware? Well, first, we need to realize we're operating on autopilot most of the time. Most humans barely pay attention to what we're doing in *that* moment—rather, we're thinking about something else.

Most of us are either ruminating about the past or thinking about the future. And when we get triggered, we generally react automatically and justify that reaction with our own assumptions (rather than pausing before reacting). This is all normal and part of being *a work in progress*; the question is, how can we, as lawyers, worry less about negative hypothetical scenarios? How can we feel less defensive towards the world? How can we be less harsh on ourselves?

First, we need to become aware of the inner stories, narratives, and self-made Hollywood movies in our heads. For example, sometimes I know that I am running away from feelings of unworthiness when I am erratically doing a million things. My mind starts spinning. I feel anxious. Only in the past few years have I been able to catch myself in that state, pause and check in (like, *My love, are you okay? what's going on?-* type of talk with myself). Before, I wasn't able to identify this because *you can't know what you don't know*. It is only when we become aware that something is off inside of us that we can do something about it. Otherwise we're just running on autopilot, not knowing we are sabotaging ourselves.

That change has obviously taken time and work; but now that I've identified most of what my recurring narratives are, I can have an honest conversation with myself: *Do I feel unworthy because I haven't been productive today? Do I feel like I am not good enough because I made a mistake on a brief? Am I freaking out about an email I sent and haven't gotten a response to yet? Do I feel lesser because I am comparing myself to what my other colleagues are accomplishing? Am I comparing myself with a multimillionaire coach on IG? Did I stay in a situation that I wanted to leave? What is it, exactly?*

Here's the thing. If you don't know what's going on, you can't do anything about it, so self-awareness is always the first step. By being self-aware, you can start to observe yourself and the stories in your head.

2) Two ways through which we can develop self-awareness are journaling and meditation. For example, if you close your eyes for five minutes and turn inward, you might start becoming aware of what your thoughts are (e.g., "*This is so annoying, aaargggg not even useful*" "*I am so hungry…*" "*I just remembered I have to do XYZ this afternoon*"). When you turn inwards, what are your thoughts like? What's your inner judge telling you? Is it telling you that "you are terrible at this meditation thing"? Is it telling you that you shouldn't apply for that job you saw earlier because you don't meet every single requirement? Is it coming up with a list of "cons" as to why you shouldn't take a risk on doing X thing?

We're going to do a mini-meditation as an ice-breaker. If you're in a public place, try to put some headphones on and look down. Turn your attention inwards as much as you can. If you're at home, close your eyes and put a 1-min timer. Breathe and observe your mind. Come back to the page when you're done 👌

[. . .]

How did that feel? Were you able to observe some of your thoughts? Were you surprised? There's no right or wrong way to do this. There's just *doing it*, and you did it. For now, since this is a book and not a workshop, we're going to focus on written self-discovery. That is, you're going to study yourself through introspective journaling.[122]

The following prompts are designed to allow you to start identifying your recurrent narratives, inner critic, or autopilot thinking:

122 For the skeptics out there (I get it, I am a lawyer too!), several studies show that both journaling and meditation improve self-awareness, resilience and emotional management. *See e.g.*, Stefanie P. Spera et al., *Expressive Writing and Coping With Job Loss*, 37 No. 3 ACADEMY OF MANAGEMENT J. 722, 722-733 (1994).

- ***For students:*** Imagine you get cold-called in class and you kind of mess up because there was one question you didn't feel too sure about. *What do you tell yourself? How do you feel about it?* Write it all down.

I tend to tell myself that mistake is going to cost me, I make everything cut-throat. I also tell myself I am not smart or that I do not belong among these smarter people.

- ***For lawyers:*** Imagine you just submitted a brief before the Court, an email to a client, or an article for a talk you'll be giving soon; and you just realized you missed something, or you weren't truly satisfied with the end result. *What do you tell yourself? What scenarios are you imagining as a result of your small "mistake"?* Write it all down.

Whatever you wrote tends to reflect what your automatic thinking (and inner critic) generally looks like. I once did this exercise with a group of lawyers and their responses were all tainted with perfectionist-autopilot rumination, such as "*I always mess up*" "*I am not as good as the other associates*" "*I won't probably get an interview - why even bother?*" "*What will my colleagues think of me?*" "*Gosh, I am the worst...*" If you haven't noticed by now, we lawyers[123] tend to be pretty harsh on ourselves. We are trained through the illusion of perfection and we're expected to reach it, even though perfection doesn't exist. We're also not "allowed" to make any mistakes, whatever their size, even though we're humans (and it is human to make mistakes).

If we become aware of our internal narratives and autopilot, we can stop the vicious cycle of self-loathing. And once we've become aware of that detrimental thinking, we can go on to the next level: reframing the narratives to our advantage. In other words, we can reframe our thinking and limiting beliefs into more compassionate and supportive ones. But before we move on, here are a couple more self-awareness-related journaling[124] prompts for deeper (and necessary) uncovering:

---

123 Unfortunately, as most humans, and not just lawyers, we tend to be overly harsh on ourselves.

124 Reminder: please take your time with all these exercises. Do them at your own pace and let your responses be as long or short as you want them to be. But if you suddenly feel inspired and the space provided herein is not enough, grab a piece of paper and allow yourself to keep going. There's no wrong or right way to do this. If you're feeling like the questions are too heavy, just leave them for now, and consider them at another time. Finally, know that you can always throw away the extra piece of paper (not the book, lol) if you're worried about privacy. The goal here is to put your answers and inner narratives on a tangible medium (e.g., voice notes would work too), so that you can become aware and conscious of them.

- **How do you feel about yourself when you don't have a productive day? What exactly do you say to yourself? Do you start feeling unworthy, or do you remain content, telling yourself that productivity fluctuates?**

I feel unsuccessful, like I am stuck in a loop of mediocraty. I hate feeling average or lazy.

- **How do you react when you make a mistake (or weren't perfect at X task)? Do you beat yourself up? What exactly comes through your mind in those moments when you've made a mistake?**

Depends on the Situation, the bigger / more important the task, the more I beat myself up. I tell myself I am an idiot and unworthy of even having the opportunity to complete the task in the first place.

- **Do you compare yourself to others? If so, can you think of a few examples where you compared your life, accomplishments, or image to others'?**

I have in the past, primarily in baseball careers and money

Reframing the narratives with a growth mindset and self-compassion

*

Do you allow yourself to make mistakes?

1) First, and foremost, we have the power to reframe and transform our self-sabotaging narratives and habitual ways of thinking—all thanks to neuroplasticity. Neuroplasticity is the brain's ever-changing ability to create what we call "synapses" or new connections between cells. These connections allow us to learn, process information and create memories. They become either weaker or stronger depending on the flow of information between them. Therefore, if our automatic thinking is always too harsh or lacking in compassion, that type of thinking (or self-loathing) will become stronger and more persistent. But just as we make that automatic thinking stronger, we can also make it weaker by adopting another way of thinking that is more beneficial for us. Think of synapses as roads you drive on.

Neuroplasticity gives us this opportunity to rewire our brains and shift the way we think or feel to more positive, supportive ways of being. And while this requires significant inner work (no, there's no magic pill), it is a powerful way to heal and transform ourselves. Thus, if every time we engage in negative self-talk we become aware of it and bring it back to our breath, we're temporarily stopping the rumination.[125] We are, in fact, disrupting that synapse or "rumination road" and taking a new road—one paved with neutrality, or even better, self-kindness. And the more we do it, the easier it will be to get to the better road because we're strengthening the neuro-connectivity it needs for that to happen.

For example, imagine you get cold-called in class. Minutes later, you automatically label the event. You either label it as positive/neutral: "*I survived a cold call! Plus, cold calling has nothing to do with my potential as a lawyer*"; or as negative: *"Oh my God. I just embarrassed myself in front of everybody. I failed at all the questions. Jesus, I am not smart enough. My classmates will think I am an idiot... What am I even doing in law school?"*.

If you choose the first road, you will experience a positive or neutral psychological response in return (and suffer less). If your brain chooses the second one, you'll likely go on a self-loathing trip (as seen through the data in previous chapters, first-year law students take the second—negative—road very often). The recorded responses[126]we saw in the Anxiety Psychoeducation Pilot program are illustrative here. As a refresher, these were some of them:

- *"I feel inadequate.*
- *I feel shame, embarrassment.*
- *I feel inferior to everyone.*
- *I felt exposed.*
- *I was the one admissions error.*

125 Okay, "every time" is a bit unrealistic because we will not be able to become aware of our thought patterns in every single instance, but the times we do are definitely a cause for celebration.

126 *Anxiety Psychoeducation, supra* note 48, at 125-26 (noting individual responses from law students).

- *I felt stressed—like I'm in a hole I can't climb out of.*
- *I feel disappointed in myself.*
- *I feel angry at myself/full of self-loathing.*
- *I feel isolated.*
- *I feel stupid.*
- *Everyone thinks I am stupid.*
- *______ [the instructor] thinks I'm an idiot; I can forget about getting any recs from her ever."*

And here is how many students would feel on the next day after being cold-called:

- *"I want to avoid everyone.*
- *I play it over obsessively in my mind.*
- *I think about all the things I should have said.*
- *I go over the case in my head so much it's not healthy.*
- *I'm mediocre.*
- *I'm less likely to raise my hand or participate next time.*
- *The next time I mess up in class it will be twice as bad.*
- *I won't be able to sleep tonight."*

I repeat this because if you're a student, I want you to know that you're not alone. Seeing recurrent narratives from real people also helps in becoming aware of them and thereby manage our own. But how can we manage our automatic thoughts?"

Short answer: by developing a mindset rooted in ongoing growth and compassion for yourself. *Long answer:* you can't suddenly eradicate the way you think in the sense that you've probably been thinking that way since your childhood, but you can reframe it repeatedly. For someone who is expected to be perfect at all times and make no mistakes, a growth mindset and a reasonable dose of self-compassion will go a long way. Those are the two concepts we'll work with in this section.

When someone has a **growth mindset**, it means they integrate failure and difficulty as an opportunity for growth. They understand that their abilities can be developed over time, and that they can—and will—improve. The opposite of a growth mindset is a fixed mindset. People with fixed mindsets see errors or mistakes as "final," and believe they're either smart, or they're not.

In a sense, a fixed mindset doesn't allow for in-betweens (e.g., *I'm smart with reading, but I can use some improvement with accounting*). Rather, it forces a black-or-white, extremist conclusion (e.g., *I'm just the worst when it comes to numbers*). Unfortunately, law school and the legal profession continue to embrace a fixed mindset most of the time. As explained throughout this book, perfectionism—and barely making any mistakes—is one of the pillars of a lawyer's identity.

Through the cold-calling system, students are expected to "know everything" about a case, even though their professors have not explained the cases to them in advance. Given the intrinsic competition at school and within the field, it is also very rare that a person will admit that they don't know X concept, or that they need to improve their skills on it. What generally happens is that in public, lawyers will act as if they know all about X, and then privately spend thousands of hours educating themselves on the issue in order to look 'perfect' on the outside. This is a survival mechanism and a consequence of a legal educational system that does not embrace vulnerability, resilience, and growth-based attitudes.

Self-compassion is another key element in reframing our internal narratives. Kristin Neff defined self-compassion as a three-fold concept consisting of (1) Mindfulness, (2) Common humanity, and (3) Self-kindness.

Therefore,[127] (1) instead of identifying with the statement *"I am unworthy, mediocre or stupid"* at a given moment, the self-compassionate person doesn't over-identify with the emotion and turns it to "*I am experiencing unworthiness right now*"; moreover, (2) that person also acknowledges that she is not alone in her struggle because there are other humans on Earth who share that struggle as well (thereby experiencing a sense of community); and finally, (3) instead of being overly harsh or self-judgmental, a self-compassionate person mothers herself when she is going through a difficult situation: *"This is hard... but I'm doing my best. It's going to be okay. I also know that I'm not alone in this pain, and there's nothing wrong with me. I'll make it out just fine."*

As you can see, factor #3 is like a mother or a friend, tenderly supporting and empowering her child or best friend—which is exactly what we need to do with ourselves.

2) Let's practice. Think of a difficult event you underwent recently.[128] Write two columns, like these ones below; and follow the instructions in brackets:

127 Here comes the application of the rule to the facts! Lawyer-talk be like...hehe.

128 It can be as simple as a cold call, a difficult case, an abusive boss, etc. Whatever you want to work with is good, but try not to pick something too heavy or too traumatic for this exercise. I also recommend you choose something you're dealing with at the moment so that it's easier to refer to.

Inner critic	Highest self
[First (and after you've identified the difficult situation you want to work with), write what your inner-critic and automatic thoughts are or were on that event—i.e., how exactly you felt about yourself and how you're interpreting the event. Try to be specific.] You were never good enough at baseball, a bust, fluke, you simply just fell short of expectations.	[Second, write from the perspective of someone who loves you and admires you deeply. That is, what would that person tell you? You can also write from the perspective of your highest self if you prefer that term.] You had such a good career filled with ups-and-downs, you got a free education, offered by MLB teams, and made life-long friends.

Inner critic	Highest self

Do you spot any significant differences? All of my students and clients have. I do, as well. Sometimes I get so caught up in perfectionistic (and merciless) expectations of myself and my work, that I become a very mean person towards myself. I suddenly forget the resilience, skills and potential I have; and I focus on the mistake, or the "failure." If I let my inner critic run freely, I'd consider myself a mediocre, not-good-enough writer/lawyer/partner/etc in a given moment of struggle. But no, that's not the truth. I am a worthy human being who is constantly growing—and so are you.

Gentle disclaimer: inner work[129]generally takes a lifetime, but it's so worth it!

Second exercise: I call it "Medicine for the perfectionist mind" and it's designed for those moments when you're judging yourself for not reaching standards of perfection.

Please pick something you're currently learning *and* struggling with, and respond to the following questions:

129 Healing is a lifelong process, especially when we're dealing with childhood traumas and systemic injustices. Yet, we have the immense powers of resilience and neuroplasticity to rewire most of ourselves—and that is a blessing. Also, healing takes place through small, everyday changes and acts of self-compassion like the ones I am suggesting here (aka be patient with yourself).

1. Rationalize

a. Are you setting unrealistic or unreasonable expectations for yourself? That is, are you new to this skill/situation you're in? Are you expecting yourself to master this new or complex thing, *right away*?

[ ] Yes [ ] No [✓] Maybe

b. Do you expect a baby to learn how to walk right away or do you give it time and patience to learn how to walk? Why?

You give them time and are patient because it is a developed skill; it takes time.

2. Practice self-compassion

Make a list of nice little actions that make you feel good below:

- *E.g., make myself a cup of tea, cuddle with my cat, listen to music, dance, swim in the ocean. . .*
- Hang out with Elle or mom
- Fish
- Watch youtube
- Lay down
- Thrift
- Shoot guns
- Drink some beer and laugh w/ friends
-

Save this list. When you're feeling uncomfortable, angry, or upset that you're not mastering the thing right away, take a deep breath and pick a very small action to nourish yourself and your body (e.g., make yourself some tea, take a break, go for a walk—whatever nourishes you from the above list). If you can't do it right away, save that little thing for the end of your day. The point is this: offer yourself the same patience and tenderness you would to a baby.

In fact, you're your baby.

3. Reinforce

Give your rational brain some affirmation magic to seal the deal. You can write your own affirmations, or use these as examples. Bring back to your mind the situation you picked, fill in the blanks, and say the affirmations to yourself.

- Progress is better than perfection.
- I don't need to be perfect in ______________
- I give myself the time and space to learn ____________
- I allow myself to make mistakes. I'm human.
- I can do complex or new things that take me some time, such as _____________

Follow this framework when you are learning a new skill or when you feel angry/bad about yourself if you don't get it right away. As a perfectionist, I used to feel stupid when I didn't understand something immediately, or when I made a mistake (I still do sometimes). I wouldn't say it aloud, but I would feel the discomfort inside. I felt that way because my perfectionism expected me to get everything right, *always*. It expected me to not make any mistakes, period; and when I say mistakes I mean the tiniest thing that, for some people[130]wouldn't be such a big deal. But as I started my healing journey, I realized that many times I didn't dare to try new things out of fear that I would fail or not be good at it right away. I realized I was often engaging in self-loathing when I didn't get things fast enough. Unfortunately, this wasn't just an isolated event; it was

130 Especially non-lawyer people.

a never-ending cycle of trying to reach perfection in everything I did. *"Did I misspell a name? Did I take longer than [insert comparison here] to figure out X task? Did I forget to cite that?*]. But guess what? Perfection doesn't even exist.

One last exercise: **what does failure mean to you?** Please be 100% honest in your answer.

Many people experience failure as a shameful thing. Maybe you don't, but if you do, know this: failure means you tried. It means you dared to do something that many people were scared to do (and will mostly never do). Failure means you were brave. It means you're learning and making progress. It means you're closer to your goal and that this is just part of the process. Failure literally means growth.

And by the way, did you know that antibiotics were discovered due to an accident; or in other words, a mistake? Alexander Fleming—the microbiologist who discovered the antibiotic penicillin in 1928—was on holiday in Suffolk; and when he came back, he realized that a fungus (the Penicillium notatum) had contaminated a portion of Staphylococcus bacteria *because* he had accidentally left it uncovered. Yep, it happened *like that.*

The more aware we are about the labeling we're giving to events, the easier it gets to spot and alter our responses to that event. Interpretation matters. That doesn't mean that you won't feel like sh*t after a cold call or a bad day. But you can reframe it with compassion and a growth mindset. When you're struggling with a specific issue or event, I invite you to also apply the exercise of *inner critic vs. highest self/loved one* as well.

If you integrate a more compassionate way of thinking, you'll give yourself space and time to learn something new. You'll allow yourself to be human: make mistakes, make progress, and grow through it all. More importantly, you won't let an outdated and unsound definition of failure define you or your goals.

Before we finish this section, I'd love for you to read these affirmations again and simply witness how they feel in your body:

- ***"I am not meant to be perfect."***
- ***"I don't have to be perfect in order to be seen, loved, and recognized."***
- ***"I am allowed to make mistakes."***
- ***"I allow myself to make mistakes, learn and grow."***
- ***"I am enough, and I'm doing my best."***

How did it feel? No right answer here, just self-awareness practice. You did it—thank you.

Mindfulness & grounding for the overthinking mind

*

Do you feel like you're 'in your head' too much?

1) Mindfulness is the state of being present, conscious or aware of something. Grounding is a therapeutic technique that allows us to safely come back to our bodies (or to the earth we're part of). Why would we want to master these? Because we're always thinking. And, as lawyers, we tend to be overthinkers. Our profession rests on how well we *think* about legal issues. Our education consists of thinking in legal arguments in order to win our case. We analyze; therefore we think—deeply.

But this is obviously not just us. According to a Harvard study,[131] humans spend almost 50% of their time inside their minds; that is, thinking about something else, rather than being present with whatever they're doing in a given moment. In law school, we're taught to become rational thinkers who will anticipate the pitfalls in a case, making sure all issues have been spotted. And while that trait is necessary to be a lawyer, we need to learn how to switch it off. We need to learn how to come back to our bodies when we're thinking about something way too much. We need to learn how to stop the constant rumination. For example, if you're making coffee, are you

---

131 Matthew Killingsworth & Daniel Gilbert, *A Wandering Mind is an Unhappy Mind*, 330 Science 932 (2010).

really making it or are you thinking about the 76 things you need to get done on that day? We all tend to do the latter, even though some of us personally love the process of making a warm drink. It's still really hard to be present. So:

How do we come back to that present moment?
How do we move from our overthinking heads to our bodies?

Well, there's not just one answer. There are as many answers as there are human beings because every person is different, and each person will resonate with different activities, somatic practices, and techniques. Accordingly, there's a reason why I'm using the term grounding in addition to mindfulness. Jon Kabat-Zinn defines mindfulness as "paying attention, on purpose, and without judgment to what is happening right here, right now." Grounding, as explored above, is defined as a therapeutic technique that helps you feel safe and connected to your body and the earth. When someone with trauma is triggered, it might be very difficult for that person to exercise mindfulness and "just be" in that suffering moment of flight-fight-frozen mode. In my personal experience, what my therapist taught me is how to safely ground myself back to the present moment, rather than meditating or breathing non-judgmentally about it.

Let me give you an example. Imagine I get into an argument with someone and I get emotionally triggered. My breathing starts going really fast and my mind starts spinning. Mindfulness, in this situation, would not necessarily be the best strategy for me because it will just make me ruminate more on the event. If I applied mindfulness—as traditionally defined—I would be focusing my attention on my thoughts and sensations, "just as they are." And while that's useful when I'm not triggered, when I am, my body doesn't feel safe because my amygdala is literally screaming *'Alarm! Danger! Run away!'*—so I would be directing a great amount of energy to alarming thoughts that produce cortisol. In those situations, what I need is to calm myself. How? Well, by grounding myself, that is, doing something that tells my body that *we're safe*. Maybe by going for a walk and feeling the breeze, or hugging myself and touching my heart, I am able to come back to my body and start feeling safe again.

By this I mean traditional mindfulness doesn't have to work perfectly for everybody—that's why it's important to learn what works for you (and ideally figure that out with a therapist if you have severe anxiety or trauma). Also beware of the media. The mainstream will tell you that mindfulness is a chill person meditating. Most of the time, it will show this inaccessible, intangible concept where you see a cool, privileged individual in a beautifully decorated (and visually perfect) room, feeling this sense of "bliss." Mindfulness encompasses much, much more—and it's not linked to just meditation or a yoga class. Those are just ways some people happened to find presence (i.e., mindfulness); but it is not the only way.

Mindfulness is not just meditation. Rather, it's a state we aim to reach—and the vehicles we drive to reach it can be very diverse. Meditators or yogis concentrate on their breathing and connecting with their bodies. But you can also do that by swimming, dancing, or drinking a nice cup of coffee as well. If mindfulness is 'being in the present moment,' the question then becomes: how can we get there? Is it stretching your body, doing yoga poses, meditating or doing breathwork, taking a cold shower, watching or experiencing ASMR,[132] feeling your own skin, cuddling with your pet, watching a baby smile, feeling the texture of the sand, experiencing the water's temperature on your skin…? You see where I'm getting at. The key is to find what works for you, not to do what everybody else on IG is doing.

First, I'll give you a brief list of things that have worked for me and the people I know. Then I'll give you an exercise for you to reflect on what techniques resonate with you and *your own, unique, human fabric.* Mark with an X, if any of the examples below resonate. If not, no worries; the next exercise will help you dive deeper. The following are activities that may create a sense of deep presence:

- Yoga [ ]
- Meditation [ ]
- Shaking, somatic movement [ ]
- Creating things with your hands [X]
- Singing [ ]
- Dancing [ ]

132 Autonomous sensory meridian response (ASMR) is a tingling sensation in response to a stimulus, which generally helps you feel more relaxed. For example, hearing the sound of pages turning, someone whispering, the tapping on a keyboard, envisioning you're at the doctor and you're receiving a great amount of personal attention, etc. There are a million ASMR videos on Youtube, and people anecdotally report that ASMR helps them greatly with anxiety. There aren't many studies yet, but this is a growing area and there will be soon. I personally love cinematic ASMR, office sounds, and personal attention. But apart from watching Youtube videos, I try to apply ASMR in real life, that is, if I am writing on a piece of paper, I try to focus on the sound of my pencil, on the turning of the pages, and so on.

- Climbing a mountain, hiking, surfing, or a demanding physical activity. . . [ ]
- ASMR in real life [ ]
- Observing nature [X]
- Taking a hot bath or shower [X]
- Drinking your favorite cup of coffee or tea [ ]
- Being with your pet [ ]
- Praying [X]

Again, these are just examples!

2) Can you think of **specific moments or activities that make you feel grounded, connected to your body or simply focused on what you're doing in that present moment?**

- Intense deep breath
- Silence
- Rubbing neck and face
- Walking outside alone
- Working out
-
-
-

If you identified an activity/ies that ground you or help you experience presence, answer the following:

1. Do you practice that activity/ies in your daily life (e.g., during the week?)

   Yes [ ] No [ ] Sometimes [X]

2. If not or sometimes, how can you add one of these activities (<u>or a fraction of it</u>) into your routine or daily schedule? Write how and what specific amount of time you can realistically dedicate to the moment or activity per day (e.g., 1 min, 5 min, 20 min).

   a. ***How exactly will you create space for that moment?*** *Example: I'm going to wake up 10 min early every day to meditate or read a book; I will schedule a short walk once a week with a friend, etc…*

      - I will spend 10 minutes at the
      - beginning of each day with breath
      -
      - I will walk at night 3 days a week

   b. ***A realistic amount of time you'll dedicate to it:*** *Example: Anything from 1-2 min to 10-min depending on the day* (remember, small, realistic, and consistent actions are the key!).

      -
      -
      -
      -

Note: you don't have to fully complete this list or exercise right now—or the other ones, as a matter of fact. You can come back to any of it, whenever you feel like it. You might not know how to respond yet, and that's okay. Trust that the answers will slowly come to you. As you read this chapter (or anything else, really), I want you to keep one thing in mind: take what resonates and leave what doesn't. Period. Everybody will try to tell you *this* or *that* is the way (*Buy this online course because this will give you happiness!).* But in reality, they're just selling *the* way that worked *for* them. We always want *the* solution, but you need to try things and find what works for you. You'll ultimately gather enough information from different sources and select what sparks your soul—that is, what gives you inner peace and what makes you feel empowered. Follow that, because if you do, you will find your own concept of mindfulness and happiness. And that's the point of it all.

<u>One last exercise</u> before we move on to the next category.

Believe it or not, sometimes it's easier to take care of others than taking care of ourselves. So, with that in mind, let's work on self-care a bit.

- **Think of two people you admire for their self-caring skills. What exactly do they to take of themselves? How do they do it?** Write everything that comes to mind.

1.

2.

Finally, **choose one self-care habit those people have, or a new one you would love to integrate in your life, and commit to exercising it at least once every two months.** It can be a very simple thing such as a watching your favorite show or going for an ice cream. It doesn't matter, whatever nurtures you consistently.

-

Boundaries: saying no & managing energy leaks

*

Do you find it hard to say no?
Or do you feel drained and depleted?

1) The message or definition here is clear: *no*. N-o. F*ck no, for my millennials and Gen Z babes. Saying no to things that drain your soul or make you feel depleted. That is another key skill to navigating life and work. Unfortunately, the legal profession is plagued with this "hustle" culture where we need to say yes to every assignment or activity so that we feel "busy enough," meaning "worthy enough." As we saw, constant busyness among lawyers is glorified—though, paradoxically, the other side of that coin is called burnout.

On a practical level, if you're saying yes to things when you don't have time for them (i.e., overextending) or when those things drain you to the point of depletion, then you're engaging in self-sabotage. I'm obviously talking about things that you can realistically say no to (but you choose to say yes to).

2) Let's do some digging. Grab the pen and let yourself write feely on the following prompts.

- **What activities/situations do you frequently say yes to, but you don't really want to?**

Shopping with Elle, family functions, extra chores around the house, washing dishes... lol

- **Why do you say yes to those? [i.e., what stories are you telling yourself about why you need to say yes or you can't say no.]**[133]

Responsibitity, sometimes you have to do shit you don't want to do, part of life

133 The typical one is "I'm a bad person if I say no to X…"

- **When you hear the words "drained and depleted," what things or moments in your life come to mind?**

College baseball career, Showing up to the field every day

- **How long does it take you to recover from draining events/moments (e.g., hours, days, weeks)? What does your recovery process look like?**

Days, I usualy let myself just embrace the struggle and treat myself with small things, rest, food etc.

- **List specific things that you would like to say *no* to (and would be able to). With each, write the specific steps/ process you would take to say no.**
  - o *Situation I'm ready to say no to:*
    - ▪ *Steps to take*:
  - o
    - ▪
  - o
    - ▪
  - o
    - ▪

In addition to unrealistic standards of perfection that lawyers are at times held to, there is the added element of emotionally dealing with clients *and* their problems. In this regard, setting boundaries also becomes a valuable skill. For example, those lawyers in the public sector or students in law school clinics who work with vulnerable clients are often at risk of experiencing empathic burnout—a term studied by researcher Tanya Singer and her team at the Max Planck Institute.

By being in constant contact with the suffering of others, our brains might start to "feel like" those who are in pain. When we compare the neural activity of a person experiencing actual pain with that of a person merely observing that person in pain, the same brain regions (the anterior insula and the anterior medial cingulate cortex) are activated in both individuals. I'm sure you've watched a really sad movie and felt this phenomenon.[134]

Let's take Carlos, who is a public defender. His client has been raped, abused, and tortured in the past; and now she's a drug addict facing possession charges. If Carlos empathizes with his client (and he has learned that he needs to, in order to "zealously advocate" for her), how will he protect himself from empathic burnout? Note that Carlos has a huge caseload of clients and crises to take care of. In order to avoid feeling the pain, will he numb himself as a defense mechanism to keep going, or will he know how to detach in a healthy way?

Well, the most common reaction in this hypothetical scenario is to emotionally check out for the sake of making it through the day. Interestingly, this is not that simple for highly empathic people, who generally end up absorbing all of their client's pain like a sponge; and instead of numbing their feelings, they just end up feeling depressed or burned out at the end of the day or week. The truth is, disengaging in the form of numbing—that is, by not emphasizing at all with the client and remaining closed off completely—is sometimes the only way we can stay focused in a profession that demands 24/7 productivity. The problem is that numbing ourselves continuously is detrimental for our mental health and, of course, for the vulnerable client, who is also suffering the side effects of her

134 Tania Singer, The Empathic Civilization: The Race to Global Consciousness in a World in Crisis (1st ed. 2010).

lawyer's detachment. While the lawyer might not necessarily suffer as much as the client, that lawyer is in deep emotional pain as well.

If, on the other hand, Carlos had been taught emotional intelligence skills while in law school, this scenario could be quite different. Carlos, who is now a public defender with a strong emotional foundation, knows that he can set healthy boundaries to protect himself from empathic distress. He understands that he is not a bad person for doing so. Rather, he knows this is a necessary step for his work to feel fulfilling and sustainable. By imposing healthy boundaries, he knows he can both empathize with clients and protect himself.

For example, he knows how to place limits—in space, time, or form—with those clients. And instead of burying the pain as a result of constantly listening to the traumatic events his clients have been through, Carlos knows how to create the moment or space to decompress and release his feelings (e.g., by writing, doing a purposeful meditation, talking to someone about it, going for a walk, or whatever he needs in order to give himself the space to do so).

When I was a detention attorney in Arizona, I would cry most days on my way home (the detention centers were an hour away from Tucson so I had plenty of time to reflect on the horrific stories of trauma survivors). I remember many of my colleagues would take calls from clients during the weekend. Some would give clients their personal phone numbers. And while some clients were very vulnerable and at risk, those lawyers were not therapists or social workers. They were human beings with huge caseloads and a need for rest. Here is the thing. When we don't know how to set healthy boundaries, we often put our clients' lives on our shoulders. And of course, every time I now write an asylum appeal I feel responsible for that person's life—I'm not a rock. I know that they can ultimately be deported to their country and possibly killed by gangs.

There's that pressure inside my head. However, I balance it out with boundaries and self-compassion. First, I don't control what a court will decide. All I can do is put my best foot forward—that's it. Second, I set boundaries around the time I dedicate to the appeal, allowing myself the space and time to decompress when feeling overwhelmed. Third, I know that putting all that emotional weight on my shoulders would just take me to one place: burnout. And I don't like that place. I don't want to be burned out because I want to continue to do the type of work I find fulfilling. As lawyers, we can be compassionate towards others and still put ourselves first.[135] These are not mutually exclusive. Setting boundaries (in time, form or space) and practicing self-compassion are necessary elements in this type of work. They're not just concepts that you learn in a psychology class you took in college. These are necessary skills for emotionally taxing legal work.

Here is an exercise to start setting some boundaries at work:

- If you are a law student or lawyer who works with vulnerable clients (or any type of client), **what are specific ways in which you could place boundaries with them?**

135 Easier said than done, of course. Ideally, when you're working with vulnerable clients on a daily basis, it can be extremely useful to have a therapist—or continuous training in this regard—to feel supported.

Examples. . .

- *I don't take calls after 6 pm or during weekends*
- *I warn my clients that I have a 48-hr window to reply to their emails*
- *Before taking a client or a case, I pause and take some time to reflect, instead of saying yes right away*
- *Before saying yes to another commitment, I ask myself: do I really have to/want to, and why?*
- *I don't talk to clients from 9 am - 2 pm because that's when I focus on research and writing, etc.*

Your turn:

-
-
-
-
-

Finally, we're going to do an exercise to manage energy leaks. The truth is, sometimes we unconsciously surround ourselves with people and situations who drain us because we are not aware of the drain. To avoid this, I like to do something I call *Energy Investment 101. Tan, tan, tan! Drumroll, please…* are you investing your energy wisely these days? Let's see:

- **Who, in your environment, indirectly or directly puts you down? Can you establish some boundaries with this person?**

No one, I don't surround myself with people like that

- **Who, in your environment, accepts you no matter your mood? How do they make you feel?**

Mom, Izzy, Elle, Travis, Doug, Jared. They make me feel secure and solid

- **Who, in your environment, supports your dreams? How?**

Mom, papa, Izzy, Mark, Elle
Friends... they assue me that the
path I am on is the path God has
chosen for me

- **As of this month/year, what situations currently drain you? Which ones nurture you?**

For literally most of my life, I spent countless hours and energy in situations that weren't empowering to my soul. I spent most of my time pleasing people. Performing for acceptance or validation. Trying to fit in. I spent time in situations that drained me or with people who subtly put me down—consciously or unconsciously. It was only recently that I finally gave myself the right to outgrow people and situations. Why? Because I deserve inner peace, inspiration, and emotional abundance in my daily life—and so do you. It just takes a little work.

Alignment: discerning what matters to you

*

What is your definition of success?

1) The final pillar we'll go over is alignment. In yoga, alignment means doing a pose in a way that benefits each individual and their *unique* bodies (from a functional perspective, not an aesthetic one). Logically, each person's alignment will depend on that person's specific body. The same thing happens with an individual's definition of success.

We tend to see success as this uniform concept, but it's not. For one person, success might mean money, prestige, and fame. For another, it might mean professional fulfillment. For others, it might mean inner peace and presence. And so on. Many of us started our careers with the definition of success our parents had predetermined for us; and it takes time to decondition yourself from aspects that might no longer resonate with what you truly value in life. Finding true success is an ongoing process.

2) So, to start that process, I'm going to ask you to close your eyes and do a 1-2 min meditation. After you read the instructions below, you'll put a 1-2 min timer and close your eyes.

Once you close your eyes, I want you to visualize your highest or successful self (i.e., who is in a complete state of contentment). Once you've visualized yourself in this state of mind, I want you to start asking yourself the questions below. After the timer ends, open your eyes and write down as much as you can remember. *Note*: This exercise is best done with a trusted friend who can guide you, ask you each question, and take notes as you describe what you're visualizing. These are the questions:

Where are you?

What are you wearing?

What are you doing?

What do you smell?

Do you feel any texture on your skin?

What things do you see around you?

What things are making you feel this way?

Is there anything else you're seeing and are excited about?

Your written notes:

*136

136 I learned this exercise through one of my early coaches, Ani. It's also a very common visualization technique that many teachers use to help people connect with their true essence. If it inspires you, share it with someone you love. That way, we expand the chain of favors and multiply the aligned people in this world.

Here are some other journaling prompts to explore your own definition of success.

- **If money[137] wasn't an issue, what lights you up, truly?** Let yourself write freely here and try not to censor yourself by analyzing whether that's possible or not right now, etc.

Honestly, being a cowboy/ ranch hand, tending to animals, hunting, fishing...

137 Yes, I'm serious! Just take money out of the equation for the sake of this exercise please :)

- **If you were to pick people you consider to be healthy, content and fulfilled in their professional and personal lives, who are they and what traits do they have that make you admire them?**

1.

2.

3.

- **Finally, if you were to define "success," what would the definition contain?** Let yourself write freely here; nobody is going to proofread it; the point is for you to sincerely let yourself flow through it.

Part iv

•

Reforming legal education

*

*

It is not the strongest of the species that survives, nor the most intelligent, but the one most responsive to change.

— Charles Darwin

Too cliché? Maybe, but change is inevitable. I also want to emphasize that the terms change or reform have no negative connotations in this book. They do not constitute an "attack." To the very contrary, change is the only constant in human life; and this chapter advocates for institutional change as a means for growth and improvement—especially in order to overcome the mental health crisis our legal profession continues to face. As such, reform represents a means to reach the collective good of all lawyers—future and present.

In chapter 8, we saw the changes that can be made on an individual level (i.e., using emotional intelligence skills to better navigate life and the practice of law). However, you and I both know that change needs to happen at the structural and institutional level, as well; otherwise, we'll continue to see the same mental health data on law students and lawyers we've been seeing for the past seventy years.

Think of it as a child being the law student/future lawyer and the parent being the law school itself. A child can indeed work on his own emotional intelligence skills in order to protect his mental health, but if the parents—that is, the institution he's inside of—don't support him, or even unconsciously contribute to his mental suffering, that child will not be able to thrive. He might *survive*; but even if he does, the path to happiness will be much harder for him as compared to a child whose parents were supportive and compassionate from the beginning. Do you see the difference?

Law schools are the ultimate incubators of all the future lawyers in the entire world. With some minor exceptions, one needs to go to law school in order to become an attorney. Accordingly, law schools hold a unique position in any lawyer's career; and they can therefore create lasting and positive change in it. And of course, law school is not the only institution that needs to change. Law firms and legal organizations need to change too; but this book is dedicated to starting at the first level of any change: education.

Law firms[138] are companies, not educational institutions. And while law schools are arguably multibillion-dollar non-profit or for-profit organizations as well, they are still considered educational institutions. As such, the pressing question here is, how can law schools create healthy and lasting change in the legal profession? How can they raise a generation of healthier, emotionally intelligent lawyers?

There is, and will always be, a multifaceted answer to this big question because the healing of our legal profession will come from different fronts. This book, however, focuses on the seed, the root, or the first stage of becoming an attorney: law school.

More importantly, this book also responds to a mental health crisis that law students have been experiencing for a very, very long

138 The idea that the billing system is outdated—or, that at minimum, it creates a lot of suffering in the workers bound by it—surpasses the limits of this book. Though it is noted ;)

time. As such, my answer to that question (and my recommendations to law schools) can be summarized as follows:

1. ***Integrate emotional intelligence in the curriculum, and utilize teaching methods that are based on growth mindsets and compassion, not fear***—especially in the 1L year, when students suffer more. In other words, teach future lawyers to manage their emotions, to better understand themselves, and to authentically decide their paths as lawyers and agents of change. Understand that a student's EQ ("Emotional Quotient") is an integral part of their professional growth; and at a minimum, eradicate abusive or intimidating methods, and teach with compassion and growth mindsets rather than fear. Finally, differentiate from theory *versus* practice.

   Offering students a theoretical class on anxiety is useful but they need to learn—and practice—specific ways to manage it. Having one psychotherapist within the law school is great, but it only offers damage control for the law school. Focus on preventive measures, rather than reactive ones. *Chapter 9* · Emotional Intelligence as an Integral Part of the Curriculum discusses all this in a more structured way.

2. ***Create institutional support, destigmatize mental health, and modernize "Career Services"***—in order to destigmatize law students' mental health struggles, we need to empower them through validation as well as foster an environment rooted in empathy and open communication.

Moreover, it's 2023, and there are a million avenues and ways to practice as an attorney.

Become curious about students' personalities so that they can choose paths that better align with both their personal and professional goals. In addition to salary and employability, have your department invest in studying career satisfaction.

Focus on the long-term, not only on the employability report the law school will send to *U.S. News*. Understand that having data that shows X number of students were hired by BigLaw is not necessarily an indicator of success if, after three years, those students end up leaving those same firms due to severe burnout or a mental health breakdown. Be transparent about the attrition numbers for certain jobs.

As the main provider of "workers" to law firms, advocate for your students' mental health care and therefore actively represent them in the bargaining process. That is, if law firms want to participate in your *On Campus Interview* fairs, ask about the state of their firm when it comes to the mental health of their employees (see Chapter 10: **More Institutional Support**).

3. ***And of course, reflect these changes at the ground level***— not just on the law school's website. Normalize and embrace the mental health conversation.

And if these measures sound like a lot, please consider the more than two hundred thousand dollars most law schools charge students for their tuition (a number that will only go up as inflation does). As seen before, the data on law students' mental health shows a pattern of suffering and a lack of institutional support. The data on lawyers' mental health doesn't get any better. The stories of suicide, burnout, and mental breakdowns are almost normalized within the profession. This is why action is needed. While individual action is powerful (Chapter 8), we also need structural and institutional change.

On one hand, institutions are the product of the needs of the individuals and groups within it. And on the other hand, institutions modify and *mold* the permanent characters of those individuals and groups. That's how interconnected they are. In fact, an institution changes as the needs and methods of the collective change.[139]

Law schools are institutions. In fact, they are prestigious and powerful institutions which, every year, harbor and *mold* a significant number of law students, who then go on to become the permanent characters of our legal profession—future lawyers, litigators, legislators, judges, policy makers, law professors, and so on.

Therefore, when the needs of those individuals change, as evidenced by the mental health data, the institution needs to change as well. We cannot have law schools that fail to effectively respond to the current needs of the students who are being molded by them. Otherwise, we encounter the same scenario as a parent who cannot effectively care for his children. If law schools are providing an educational service that does not meet the needs of their students (i.e., clients), how can we justify the fairness of their contractual bargain?

Being proactive and responsive to change or a crisis are not easy things, but we can at least try. More importantly, we can choose to

139 Luther Lee Bernard, An Introduction to Social Psychology (1st ed. 1926).

be either reactive or proactive. If law schools take the reactive route, they will be focused on damage control and short-term solutions (e.g., just having a psychotherapist within the law school to be responsible for the mental health of the whole student body—which, by the way, is an unreasonable burden).

If, on the other hand, law schools take the preventive route, they will safeguard their students' mental health by using education and validation (i.e, emotional training and open communication); adequate resources for their growth as professionals and human beings (i.e., Career Services departments that focus on law students' long-term success and wellbeing); as well as care-based systems that foster a collaborative and healthy environment where vulnerability is not a liability, but a skill (i.e., communal healing or community-based support, wellbeing resources, group therapy, etc.) As the 2021 Survey of Law Student Well-Being emphasized:

> It is the authors' hope that the findings will continue to urge legal education stakeholders to prioritize mental health and wellness for law students.[140]

The time to do so is now.

140 *2021 SLSWB Study*, *supra* note 31, at 9.

9

Emotional Intelligence as an Integral Part of the Legal Curriculum

If you find it in your heart to care for somebody else, you will have succeeded.

— Maya Angelou

I don't have *the ultimate answer* to our huge problem. But I have spent countless hours researching, studying and training myself to be able to help my legal community—past, present, and future. Yet, this is not about me or this book. It's about a deeply flawed system that is creating suffering for many. And one thing is for sure: emotionally educating law students is a significant part of the solution. Law students and lawyers need emotional tools to survive and thrive; and not providing them with those tools is doing them a disservice. With that in mind, scholars asked the following:

> If law schools are not in the business of preparing students for the practice of law, then to what do we owe its existence?"[141]

The practice of law is not emotionless.[142] To the very contrary, it will present a million situations—with clients, colleagues, judges, co-workers, and so forth—that will require the management of emotions. Consequently, we need to integrate the emotional element within legal training. But if that argument is not strong enough, consider the data presented throughout this book. If law students are showing serious signs of anxiety and depression *after* they enroll in law school, how do we justify not providing them with the emotional tools to cope with that level of pressure and stress? More importantly, if the prospects of law students' mental health just worsen once they enter the profession, how can we justify not training them for that outcome?

141 Suzanne Valdez Carey, *An Essay on The Evolution of Clinical Legal Education and Its Impact on Student Trial Practice*, 51 U. Kan. L. Rev. 509, 509 (2003).

142 Nothing in life is.

As of today, lawyers continue to experience high rates of depression, anxiety, and isolation as compared to the general population. The results from studies conducted in the 90s and 2000s continue[143] to appear in newer studies; so we know there is a pattern. Why is this important? Because that is the legal profession—or the mental health situation—future lawyers will be entering. We have enough stories of substance abuse, anxiety-fueled breakdowns, and suicides both in law school and within law firms. The statistics are so bad that the American Bar Association had to create a full force dedicated to dealing with the alcohol abuse and mental health crisis within the legal profession! And while the profession is waking up to this issue, the question becomes:

Will we address the root of the problem,
or will we continue to react only to the symptoms?

If we decide to plant the right seeds in law school, it will mean that at a minimum, law students will receive a more compassionate, supportive, and interdisciplinary education. Here are some specific recommendations for law schools, or law students who want to advocate for change in their schools:

(1) Eliminate or minimize fear-based teaching techniques

First, eradicate or minimize the cold calling that humiliates the student in front of their peers. Without this step, the student will

143 COVID also worsened things. *See The Legal Industry's Mental Health Problem Grew in 2020, Our Survey Shows,* THE AMERICAN LAWYER, (last updated, May 3, 2021 at 5:00 am).

continue to be terrified or traumatized in class. Connected to this, instruct faculty on the negative implications of cold-calling students through a modified Socratic method that creates terror and hinders participation. Show them the studies, especially the students' testimonies. Create a feeling of empathy and have the law professors (re) position themselves in the students' shoes:

> Before the session, I felt very anxious about the prospect of cold calling, and I was very anxious whenever I was cold called in class (racing heart, difficulty concentrat[ing] on the question/thinking, etc. . . .[144]
>
> [Response from a law student in the Anxiety Psychoeducation Pilot Program].

Eliminating fear from the equation doesn't mean that law schools need to turn into flowers and rainbows. There will be pressure, stress, and challenging situations—because those are all part of being human as well as being a graduate student. What we're doing here is eliminating techniques that directly create *too much suffering* for the student without a logical justification for it; and instead, adopt a more modern and positive framework that will enhance the student's learning experience.

We're no longer in the nineteenth century, and it is therefore time to approach and design the educational process through the lens of modern psychology (or at a minimum, we ought to take into account how outdated methods are damaging our students' mental

144 *Anxiety Psychoeducation*, *supra* note 48, at 136.

health). For example, we have access to positive psychology—that is, the scientific study of human flourishing; or as Martin Seligman put it, the study of what makes life worth living, both for the individual and societal well-being. More importantly, we now know that greater wellbeing enhances learning.

Students are in law school to *learn*, not to suffer through a constant state of anxiety or unworthiness. A learning process means that one cannot be expected to know it all from the beginning. Learning entails the process of improving, making mistakes, and getting better at things. As we saw throughout this book, cold calling hinders participation—or, in other words, it steals room from questions, reflection, and growth. If, on the other hand, we teach with optimism, we help students build resilience—another pillar of emotional intelligence.

Resilience is the ability to overcome failure and difficulties, and building resilience also strengthens our growth mindset. Resilience helps us surpass the obstacles that life inevitably brings; and it also helps us accept that we don't need to be perfect human beings all the time. This skill is not only useful but necessary for that law student who didn't make it to the top of the curve, had a family emergency during exam period, or is having difficulty understanding legal concepts. Likewise, self-compassion and a growth mindset are extremely useful for that perfectionistic, overachieving law student. Remember what we talked about earlier on the difference between a fixed and a growth mindset?

In this regard, Dweck emphasized how a culture of praise for effort, strategy, and improvement would allow space for resilient individuals. In her TED Talk,[145] Dweck also mentioned a study that can be directly applied to the law school classroom. In that study, her research team separated two groups of students. To the first group, the researchers directly taught them the concept of a growth mindset—that is, the fact that every time students pushed themselves out of their comfort zones, their neurons formed new and stronger connections, which over time, could make them smarter. To the second group, however, the researchers did not mention any of this. When they compared the two groups during a school transition, the second group's grades had declined while the first—growth mindset group—had a strong rebound in their grades.[146]

For example, in those law schools with a grading curve, we can also start by honestly explaining to 1Ls how the 1L curve exactly works, so that when grades come out they don't think they have "failed." When teaching them a growth mindset, we can emphasize that their grades are not some unfixable failure or mistake that will follow them for the rest of their legal careers. More importantly, we can teach them that a resilient, growth mindset is a trait they can certainly use as they encounter difficult cases and situations throughout their careers. And as some law professors thankfully do, we can

---

145 Carol Dweck, *The Power of Believing that You Can Improve*, TED (Nov. 2014) https://www.ted.com/talks/carol_dweck_the_power_of_believing_that_you_can_improve?language=en.

146 During the TED Talk, Dweck also talks about a study conducted at the University of Washington, where her team created an online math game that rewarded "yet" and "not yet" instead of "right" or "wrong." They discovered that the students who put in more effort, more strategies, and more engagement over a longer period of time were also more likely to do so when they encountered more complex math problems. By changing the concepts to growth-based terms such as "yet" and "not yet," the kids were developing greater confidence and persistence. *See e.g.*, Jo Boaler, Mathematical Mindsets: Unleashing Students' Potential through Creative Math, Inspiring Messages and Innovative Teaching (1st Ed. 2016).

encourage participation in class, rather than intellectually attacking first-year students in front of their peers. To cite Law Professor Huang, "[in order to] give students the tools of optimism, professors can embed optimist language into their courses, and law schools can also teach resilience."[147] At minimum, it is time to move towards a model that teaches with curiosity, compassion, and understanding, rather than fear.

(2) Make Emotional Intelligence a required, integral, core part of legal training

The legal educational system in its present form exclusively emphasizes objective thought, rational deduction and empirical proof. While this mental training is important for intellectual growth, the rational overemphasis results in the student developing *zero to little* emotional skills. Accordingly, we need to integrate a required class that teaches students Emotional Intelligence (EI) skills. There are a couple of important points here.

Interactive and taught with compassion:

A core class in Emotional Intelligence cannot be solely theoretical—it needs to be interactive, as we saw in Chapter 8. Law students already have enough texts to read, so this training is not about adding 50 pages of anxiety studies to their weekly assignments. It needs to be a hybrid, where the student cognitively understands what's happening in their brain (e.g., how the legal mind works or how

147 Peter H. Huang et al., *The Zombie Lawyer Apocalypse*, 42 Pepp. L. Rev. 727, 768-69 (2015).

their nervous system gets activated) and how to build the emotional skills to better navigate some of the difficult emotions they will go through in law school. Law students, as logical and sometimes skeptical thinkers, can find it useful to see the data that proves the high percentages of mental health-related problems in the law. As they acknowledge those numbers and realize that they—or someone they know—might be in those percentages, they will find credibility and an empirical justification for the instruction of this class.

Moreover, by merely teaching law students about concepts theoretically—that is, without hands-on practice, mindfulness exercises, or collaborative mediums—we are just reiterating the thinker traits that legal education already exacerbates. In other words, we're just teaching law students to 'analyze and overanalyze the issue' of mental health. Therefore, using interactive exercises that promote self-discovery, presence, and movement can prove useful for a collective who spends their day-to-day thinking and analyzing legal issues. In other words, the goal is to teach our highly analytical thinkers how to stop vicious mental cycles and how to come back to their bodies.

Examples of the interactive portion of this class can include, among others: introspective journaling, affirmation work, or mindfulness-based meditation (self-awareness, presence, and self-empowerment), breathing and other body-based techniques to calm the nervous system (self-regulation), intention-setting and peer accountability (motivation), or practicing active listening and destigmatizing mental health struggles with classmates (empathy). Whatever exercises we choose, we're focusing on raising the student's emotional quotient (EQ).

In addition, this EI class should also be a space to freely share about struggles, and therefore embrace human vulnerability. The EI's class instructor should ideally be a compassionate and empathic person. In plain terms, it is useless to have a PhD professor or a therapist with a huge resume teach this class when that person has no social or emotional skills themselves, or has a hard time connecting with students. Yes, that happens—I am sure we have all experienced the difference between a professor who is very good with research and publications, but who does not know how to teach or communicate in class.

We are looking for someone with whom students feel emotionally safe and empowered; therefore, it's crucial to have the right people teach this type of class. Again, this is not about how many publications a person has—it's about the humanity, empathy, and social skills that person exercises in their life. Students will look up to this person, so if I were a student, I would want to look up to someone who is actually a kind, aligned, and compassionate individual regardless of their list of titles—wouldn't you?

Tailored to the intricacies of the legal mind:

Moreover, the class will ideally be tailored to the legal mind and to the legal profession. That is, apart from the main pillars of emotional intelligence, such as self-awareness, self-regulation, motivation, empathy and social skills;[148]we would teach law students

148 These are the pillars defined by Daniel Goleman, who is considered the Father of Emotional Intelligence. However, this concept is ever-evolving, and as seen in Chapter 8, I've added emotional-based concepts such as boundaries, alignment, growth mindset, and self-compassion because they're directly connected to professional development and the practice of law.

about areas that are especially useful in their growth as professionals who will be in the practice of law, such as mindset/resilience, self-compassion, alignment and boundaries. The reason why these additional concepts are important is because they offset the detrimental stereotypes that can arise within lawyers, such as perfectionism, productivity 24/7, or busyness as the only measure of worth, excessive competition and comparisonitis, negative or pessimistic thinking; and of course, the overemphasis of thinker traits and the abandonment of emotional ones.

For example, self-compassion is an especially useful trait for lawyers, who are generally trained within standards of perfection, and consequently tend to be extra exigent and harsh on themselves. Since we[149] lawyers tend to be prone to self-criticism, we need to learn how to offset the negative results of that automatic pilot thinking. As we saw in Chapter 8, if we self-flagellate on something we did or did not do, we need to be able to catch ourselves—and our inner judge or critic—before we get sucked into a vicious cycle of rumination (e.g., *"Oh c'mon, you're gonna turn that thing in? It sucks!"; "You shouldn't write about that topic, you're not experienced enough... plus, I'm sure someone has already written about it"; "You forgot to mention article 7 and 8... that was so lame and speaks about what type of lawyer you are..." etc*).

Logically, if one starts believing their own self-sabotaging and self-loathing stories, their wellbeing will decrease (let alone the self-imposed limitations and loss of opportunity that those stories will create in their lives and careers). In order to help law students not

149 I'm generalizing so please don't feel offended! It's awesome if you don't have a high dose of self-criticism.

internalize perfection as a threshold for their worth, we need to teach them how to be self-conscious of these narratives as well as how to reframe them with a self-compassionate discourse. If you want to analyze whether your law student body is in need of self-compassion and a growth mindset, ask them the following questions and sum up the answers:[150]

1. If you don't know how to respond to a cold call, do you self-loath or beat yourself up? Do you tell yourself you're stupid or 'not smart'?

   [ ] Yes [ ] No [ ] Sometimes

2. Have you ever told yourself that you're not good enough to be in law school because you're no longer a top law student like you were in college?

   [ ] Yes [ ] No [ ] Sometimes

3. If you're extremely tired and need to take a break from reading, do you force yourself to keep going?

   [ ] Yes [ ] No [ ] Sometimes

150 If you use any of the teachings and exercises from this book, please kindly cite this work. Thank you!

4. Do you feel like you've sacrificed your physical and mental health since you started law school?

   [ ] Yes [ ] No [ ] Sometimes

5. When you get tired, do you feel that you're lazy or weak?

   [ ] Yes [ ] No [ ] Sometimes

6. Do you feel like you need to sacrifice your family, physical exercise, or self-care if you truly want to become a successful attorney? (Honest answer!)

   [ ] Yes [ ] No [ ] Sometimes

Self-awareness, alignment and boundaries are also important emotional areas for a law student's life and future career as a lawyer. It is only through self-discovery that one can change their habits and habitual thinking. As proposed in Chapter 8, introspective journaling can be beneficial when it comes to managing emotionally challenging situations and building resilience. Through journaling, we can also teach law students how to cognitively reframe detrimental narratives and persistent feelings of self-doubt or unworthiness—especially within the competitive environment they're in.

Once the student identifies the recurrent narratives and thoughts she is currently having (i.e., self-awareness), the student can move onto reframing and reinterpreting those internal stories using a more compassionate, resilient lens, as opposed to the perfectionistic and competitive tendencies they generally absorb in law school.[151] What matters is that the students learn how to empower themselves throughout the difficulty of their law school experience (and future career as lawyers).

It is true that concepts like self-compassion can be hard to teach to a group of highly ambitious overachievers. But the point is to position these skills as key components of long-term success. During that process, I repeat: it is important to show law students—especially the most skeptical ones—the data or information on lawyers' mental health.

In sum, EI should be a foundational, core class because it will provide the student with the tools to understand and navigate the stressors that comes with being an attorney—that is, the stereotypes that are still being embraced, the ways in which the legal mind spills over our personal lives, the restless competition in the field, the expectations of perfection, and so on. Think about how the data in the legal field will change if we raise a generation of emotionally intelligent lawyers. Can you think of how many of those will have the skills to choose a healthy coping mechanism instead of detrimental ones?

---

151 For example, take the student who got four Bs in their first semester. Instead of internalizing an inner critic of '*Well, I'm definitely not a good student anymore. And there's proof of that,*" we can teach that student to practice a supportive, resilient approach of "*I did my best within the curve. These grades don't mean that I'll be a bad lawyer. I can improve and I will keep fighting.*"

Integral and not *incidental* support:

There is a difference between having EI be an integral part of a law student's education *versus* simply offering emotional intelligence resources or elective courses to law students. Here is exactly why: given the heavy workload law students have, if a class on EI or lawyer wellbeing is not integrated as a natural part of the curriculum, law students will be forced to choose between their mental health *and* their other core classes, i.e., their 1L grades.

EI training—i.e., healthy ways to maintain their mental health—cannot represent an *additional burden* for the already overwhelmed law student. Imagine the dilemma of a 1L:

> *Should I keep reading and outlining for Torts or should I go to that emotional intelligence elective class? Is it worth trading that hour of work when my classmates—who are competing against me for grades—will use that hour to get ahead on their Torts' readings?*

Again, law school is a very competitive institution. We need to keep this in mind when we're deciding what measures to add as solutions for the mental health crisis. Electives and class offerings around lawyer well-being are great, but as long as they are not an integral part of their educational priorities, students will be disincentivized by the opportunity costs[152] these offerings present.

152 We especially need to make sure that 1Ls—the ones who tend to suffer the most—have access to this type of training early on, and especially that they are not forced to sacrifice study time from other 1L classes (or be *de facto* punished) for protecting and strengthening their mental

If studies show that law students feel the need to take unprescribed Adderall to survive and compete against other law students, do we really think that most of them will be inclined to lose a precious hour of their study time in order to care for their mental health? [Rhetorical question]. And no! We can't blame them for not doing so. It is unreasonable to place that burden on law students.

Many of these students, especially first-years, enter survival mode the minute they start the law school race. From the very first month, law school teaches students that they only have two priorities: *grades & resume.*

This message is what students interiorize because it is directly, or indirectly, sent by the institutions they're in. Likewise, second and third-year students are extremely busy building their resumes and participating in journals, competitions or clinics, so why would they pay attention to EI or mental health—i.e., an aspect that has never been emphasized to them?

If law schools don't integrate the importance of emotional intelligence and mental health in their formal training, law students will interiorize something like this:

> *Yeah, I think I've heard some stuff about mental health and emotional intelligence, but that's not important for my grades or my resume right now. That's not a priority, so I can't bother with it right now.*

---

health as their school year goes on. Hence why emotional training needs to be an integral part of the curriculum, rather than merely an optional class.

An example of this can be found in the Psychoeducation Pilot Program done by Stanford and Yale law schools that we've mentioned in this book. This was a brief cognitive behavioral model designed to help law students cope with anxiety. It consisted of *two* one-to-four-hour *meetings* and attendance was *voluntary.* One of the amazing things about this pilot program is that it (1) genuinely taught law students about the things they might experience in law school—that is, anxiety, stress, and maybe depression; and (2) it allowed them to see how other classmates felt similar things, therefore feeling validated in the stressful experience that law school can be. There was, however, an obvious limitation.

The program was designed as a one-time event, rather than a consistent program over time. We must therefore ask, is a one-time orientation or a couple of group sessions capable of creating long-lasting effects? After a year and a half had elapsed since the psychoeducation sessions, students were asked whether the teachings had stayed with them or whether they continued to use the techniques they had learned. These were some of their responses:[153]

- I don't remember which ones, nor do I consciously still use them, but the sessions generally made me more optimistic about law school.

- It's hard to remember specifics this far from the session but I think we talked about exercise, keeping up with non-law things . . .

153 *Anxiety Psychoeducation, supra* note 48, at 132-33.

- I don't specifically remember any of the techniques, but I do remember the discussions . . .

Naturally, if a new skill is not practiced, we tend to forget it and revert back to our habitual patterns. Another student wisely noted:

- **I think this is a beneficial program and would hope it is a mandatory/universal experience, and not just aimed at those who self-identify as having anxiety . . .**

Training in emotional intelligence or validating the students' mental health struggles cannot be a one-time event if we want to shift the current paradigm. It is great to mention it during orientation, but it needs to be an integral part of the curriculum, thereby functioning as an on-going process—especially for the first-year students who are more likely to experience higher levels of distress.

More importantly, if we give law students this type of training, we're investing in a more aware, empathic, and emotionally intelligent generation of lawyers who will in turn become better leaders in our society. We can reduce the use of maladaptive coping mechanisms both law students and lawyers use, such as alcohol or drug abuse. But without this type of training, we can't expect to have healthy lawyers because we have not prioritized their mental and emotional health in law school.

10

Institutional Support:

Destigmatizing Mental Health Struggles, Embracing Vulnerability, and Offering More Support

"Shame derives its power from being unspeakable."

— Brené Brown

Apart from integrating emotional intelligence in legal education as a foundational pillar for change, this chapter presents some additional thoughts on how we can continue to address the current law student mental health crisis. In connection with requiring emotional intelligence training as an integral—and not incidental—part of legal education, we also need to make it easy for the law student to stay healthy, or seek help if needed. In other words, legal education should encompass both legal know-how and an interdisciplinary aspect that supports the student while they're pursuing their law degrees.

We can start by creating spaces where we can talk openly about the mental health struggles law students go through. A great example of what a positive intervention looks like is the **peer-support** model Professor Andrew Benjamin has implemented at the University of Washington Law School. This intervention takes the form of a three-credit "Counseling Workshop" for second and third year-law students.

In this workshop, students learn to develop counseling skills, increase multicultural sensitivity, and engage as peer supporters with other law students. Unlike merely theoretical courses, this learning experience fosters empathy, hands-on practice and community-based support. As Benjamin describes it, the focus of the workshop's goal is to end isolation, provide resources to manage stress, and promote health in the study community—all necessary measures to address the mental health crisis within law schools. Specifically,

> Through active listening and situational analysis, peer counselors will help empower their fellow law students to address productively the wide-range of personal and academic challenges associated with law school. Multicultural

> engagement will remain a key approach in all interactions. Peer counselors will remain non-judgmental and will avoid applying pressure around decision-making.[154]

That is what a supportive and inclusive teaching model can look like. Furthermore, this type of workshop is both disruptive and beneficial because it counterbalances some of the negative traits law school intensifies: adversarial attitudes, emotionless perfectionism, and relentless competition between classmates—which too often lead to student's isolation and excessive individualism.

The need for vulnerability, open communication and communal healing

Moreover, and simply put, law students need to know that they are not alone in their pain. Having a safe environment where they can share how they feel—or even do so anonymously, writing their answers on a piece of paper—creates a sense of shared humanity and struggle (also a component of self-compassion). Therefore, it is crucial that law schools encourage safe and supportive conversations around the struggles law students and lawyers go through. Given the misconception or limiting beliefs that operate within law schools—such as failing or not being perfect as a sign of weakness—it is not surprising that mental health struggles, or any sign of 'weakness,' are things that are not talked about in law school. Let me tell you two stories that illustrate this point.

---

154 The class description can be accessed on the law school's official website at www.law.washington.edu under the course catalog.

Two years ago, a SJD student from Arizona Law contacted me to talk about my experience failing the Bar Exam for the first time. He had been recording peoples' stories of failing the Bar because he realized people who had failed the Bar didn't have a place to turn to for support, as most people didn't like to disclose it or talk about it. Charles Benaza created '*The Bar Stories Project*' on Youtube in order to respond to a need that was palpable in law school and in the legal profession: the transparency for the real, and not so uncommon, shared struggle of failing the bar exam.

During my talk with Charles and his colleague Lauren, I was able to share with the audience the feelings of unworthiness that generally overwhelm anybody who has failed the bar exam for the first time (or other times after that). I talked about how I went through several weeks of self-loathing and doubting my intellectual abilities, until I put myself together and hired a coach, who not only helped me pass the Arizona Bar Exam on my second attempt, but who also reminded me of my inherent intelligence and talents (*Mary Goza, thank you endlessly*).

The interesting thing was that there was barely anybody talking about these issues publicly. As if it was shameful to admit that one has failed the Bar Exam (as mentioned, Michelle Obama and John F. Kennedy failed on their first attempt; and so have many other successful people). In that sense, Charles' project was, to say the least, a miracle space for vulnerability, communication and empowerment within the legal community.

The same thing happens when it comes to academic dismissal in law school. Two years ago, a student contacted me to inquire about my coaching services. She told me that after a year of personal difficulties, she had been academically dismissed from law school. She was devastated. During our first talk, we discussed how the event had affected her sense of worth. She also mentioned that she felt shameful and alone in her pain because she could not find people who had gone through a similar experience. After a semester of coaching, this student bounced back, got admitted to another law school, and radically increased her GPA. She reframed her experience as a story of resilience and determination.

In one of our talks, she mentioned she had only heard one person talk about academic dismissal openly on Youtube—and that marvelous person is Lamarr Martin.

When I started my Instagram page 'Esperanza is Hope' [@ esperanza.ishope] to support and guide law students, I had the luck of meeting Lamarr—also known as the "Law Student Encourager" [www.lawstudentencourager.com]. His story is simply one of my favorite stories of humility, endurance, and grit. Lamarr was academically dismissed in his first year of law school and he had to wait another two years to be able to reapply to that same law school. During those two years, he worked in the post office of his law school, thereby seeing his colleagues and friends attending the classes he wasn't able to attend. Yet he waited; he persisted. Lamarr reapplied, was readmitted, and now he is a successful law student who encourages other students with his amazing and funny online videos. But again, Lamarr is an exception to the general rule of 'failure equals weakness.'

Only by bravely breaking this barrier of silence, he has been able to make a huge difference in many students' lives. Luckily, people are getting tired of superficial stories of perfection online. People want to hear the truth—the real, raw truth about the struggles we overcome in order to become who we are today.

People have an innate need to relate to other, *real* people. Though most law students frequently hide or don't talk about their struggles in law school, the data shows that their experiences are very similar to each other. As such, if we want to destigmatize these issues and encourage students to talk about them, we need to create safe spaces for them to do so. To illustrate this point, let's take one last look[155]at the responses from Yale and Stanford law students in the Anxiety Psychoeducation Pilot Program:

> Question 3: Has anything else about these [anxiety] sessions stayed with you? [Students' responses:]
>
> - The supportive atmosphere of dealing with issues and insecurities with my classmates, many of whom shared the same feelings.
>
> . . .
>
> - The session created a camaraderie within the group that has persisted. That is very valuable.
>
> . . .

155 And you might find this study repetitive, but it compiles the students' voices; and I believe it is essential to actively *listen to the people*, that is, law students and their experiences within the system.

- It was wonderful to get to know my section and my professor on a deeper level. . . and of course, just the act of talking about anxiety and realizing that your peers have similar concerns helps ameliorate the problem.

. . .

- Generally, the concept of automatic thoughts… and more than that, the sense that anxiety is something that everyone deals with. . .

. . .

- Simply knowing that I wasn't alone about anxiety and law school. Hearing Professor Fried say that she was anxious, and hearing my classmates talk about it was really refreshing.[156]

***

Being vulnerable with ourselves and others can be an immense source of power. We can loosen our grip. We can relax. We don't have to be perfect all the time. We are allowed to be human beings, because that's what we are.

156 *Anxiety Psychoeducation*, *supra* note 48, at 133.

More support through on-site resources and an updated career services department

Offering on-site counseling or facilitating stress-relief activities to law students is another way to increase institutional support. There are several law schools who are already doing this, which indicates that they're hopefully on a serious path to improving and creating a healthier educational journey for their students. That said, just offering wellbeing resources (e.g., optional meditation circles, a free yoga class, etc.) are still reactive measures to the problem we have.

For example, let's take Georgetown and its Center for Wellness Promotion, since it does a great job offering law students a wide range of services to care for physical, spiritual, and mental wellbeing. According to their website, Georgetown Law offers the following spaces and services *free of charge* to their law students:

- *Sport & Fitness Center*—open seven days a week.
- *Spirit*—programming and workshops to examine the intersection between personal values and careers in law, the definition of success, and more.
- *Mind*—which includes a co-curricular course that teaches law students mindfulness and ways to navigate stress; as well as "free online therapy for those with student health insurance."[157]

157 This information can be found on Georgetown law's official website at www.law.georgetown.edu under the tab 'Your life & Career' (emphasis added).

As the institution notes on their official website, "Georgetown is one of the only law schools in the country with on-staff therapists and a psychiatrist who offer a range of free psychological services." There's also a team that coordinates free and confidential assault and relationship services for Georgetown law students. I've taken Georgetown as an example because they tell their audience that "wellness is a foundation of academic and professional success;" but there are other law schools who are also doing a great job, as well. That said, I haven't talked to Georgetown law students and I don't know how effective and practical these resources are in real life (e.g., I don't know how many students carry health insurance or if all the therapy sessions are free and accessible, or if most of these things are very far away[158] from their law school campus), but I can see how the law school is making an effort to support the students. Another interesting model is one that offers law students discounts in various physical and creative activities outside the school.[159]

But again, law students don't have time. And while these resources are great, change still needs to happen at the very core of the legal educational framework. Most importantly, we cannot rely solely on external resources when we know that law students are reluctant to seek help. Moreover, the 2021 SLSWB study showed how financial concerns have increased as a factor discouraging or impeding law students from seeking help. Last year, I attended an online conference on law students' mental health, and this professor or administrator noted how great it was that they had one therapist

158 Once again, law students don't have time.

159 When I studied abroad in SciencesPo (Paris), they had an incredible list of offerings and activities that we could sign up for outside of the law school for a very, very affordable price (e.g., from samba dancing to ceramics…).

at the law school and that her office had a *wall* that prevented other students from seeing who was going into her office to receive therapy. Do you see the problem here?

We continue to *hide* behind a wall. While it is great that some law schools are dealing with the symptoms, we still need to move from a reactive mode to a proactive one. We need to destigmatize mental health issues, support students in their struggles, and provide them foundational skills first; not secretly offer them a therapist so that no one knows they're going through a rough time. Specifically, why not lay a strong, mental health foundation early on in order to prevent the damage? And to reiterate, emotional intelligence tools are necessary for the professional growth of a lawyer and the student who will be dealing with all of the following:

- Intense competition and high academic demands, including a grading curve in many law schools;
- Consolidation of perfectionism and the "everything is fine" collective illusion as a way of existing in the legal field (which too frequently turn into self-loathing narratives for the already overachieving law student);
- Overemphasis of lawyer only-rational, "thinker" traits, discarding (and even stigmatizing) the emotional traits a human being has; and
- Stigmatization and silent attitudes towards law students' mental health.

In sum, we should aim to move from an anxiety-inducing and intimidating environment to an educational model that enhances the student's learning experience and provides them with an emotional skillset to tackle the stressors within the legal profession. We should aim to raise a generation of healthier, more aligned, emotionally intelligent lawyers who will create lasting change in our profession.

Updating & Modernizing Career Services

Connected to alignment with one's values and the definition of success is the role of career advisors. Did you know the legal profession has birthed an incredibly solid and secondary industry that helps lawyers *quit* the law? The internet is filled with coaches and articles covering alternative careers for lawyers, how to leave the law, and all of the reasons why you should quit the practice of law and do something else. And while the exit might be the right path for some, I deeply resonate with what Professors Todd & Elizabeth Peterson stated:

> [T]he solution to the problem may be less about law firms trying to make their lawyers happier and more about ensuring that the right people are entering the right law firms to begin with, or more generally, that students are steering themselves toward the right careers.[160]

As explained in chapter 7, we need to expand the lawyer identity to match the current needs of our emotional and interdisciplinary

160 Todd David Peterson & Elizabeth Waters Peterson, *Stemming the Tide of Law Student Depression: What Law Schools Need to Learn from the Science of Positive Psychology*, 9 YALE J. HEALTH POL'Y L. ETHICS 357, 417 (2009).

personae, and to encompass the different profiles law students may have—from litigators to policy makers, mediators, conflict managers, and so on. We should aim for a career office that is able to address this variance in students' profiles as well as factor their natural predispositions into their job placements. In this regard, both Professors Peterson advocated for career counseling that was able to identify the student's signature strengths, so that such information could help the career office identify jobs that would provide the most satisfying career for each law student.

This information can be obtained by administering surveys, such as the Gallup Organization's Strength-finder Survey. This survey specifically assesses the top five strengths of an individual, out of thirty-four strength themes that are divided into four domains: strategic thinking, relationship building, influencing and executing. There are also a variety of personality assessment tools that many human resources and hiring departments at top companies use as well, such as the Myers-Briggs Type Indicator, which is a self-report questionnaire that helps a person understand how they perceive and operate within the world according to four categories: introversion or extraversion, sensing or intuition, thinking or feeling, and judging or perceiving. That said, many of these are regarded as pseudoscience and have their own limitations, so it's important that Career Services does not use them to make any final determinations. **Rather, they should focus on giving the student tools to explore their values, strengths, and interests.** In other words, the point is to help law students to get to know themselves better.

Moreover, Career Services can be more transparent about the jobs and the workplaces these students will be applying to. For a century, law schools have been raising machine-like students because this is what most law firms were asking for. But given the current mental health crisis, more and more law firms are looking for individuals who are self-aware, can manage stress, communicate in healthy ways, and can self-motivate. This means that law firms are looking for workers who *will stay*, rather than burn out and leave.

Knowing how to envision a future, in the material and emotional sphere, can encourage better, more well-informed decision making when deciding to apply for certain jobs. The more the student knows about himself, the better equipped he will be to aim for a job that will ultimately bring him what he is yearning for. This doesn't mean that Career Services is suddenly responsible for the student's career satisfaction. It merely means that it can provide the student with the tools and real information *about* career satisfaction. Plus, if the law student has learned alignment,[161] in his Emotional Intelligence core course, he will have more self-awareness on what values he wants at the core of his life. The more emotionally intelligent the student is, the higher the chances he will make better decisions regarding his work, life, and wellbeing.

Finally, Career Services departments need to live in the time their students are living in. This means studying the market and the new jobs and work modalities that appear. Take me, for example. I am a virtual lawyer who doesn't even live in the United States. I started writing appeals as a freelancer because I could not work in the US due to not having citizenship or a green card. Though I felt lonely at the beginning of my journey, I now know virtual (and young) lawyers who have their own virtual firms—especially

161 By alignment I mean to be aligned with one's moral values and definitions of fulfillment.

in practice areas that allow for remote working, such as trademark or business law.

There are also attorneys who divide their time between being lawyers and online coaches, as well. Part-time jobs are often dismissed with no real justification. There are more options than clerking or working for a law firm. Of course, if you ask me, I would have taken a federal clerkship if it hadn't been for the fact that, as a non-US citizen (or a green card holder in a couple of states), I could not be hired. But the point here is for career counselors to explore aligned options with students, expanding beyond reviewing resumes and telling students to dress up as either a woman or a man when they're interviewing for a job. The modern world, including the legal market, is constantly changing—and a department like Career Services should be on top of new trends.

CLOSING THOUGHTS

For lawyers:

Change is scary—it literally is. We (I include myself) sort of want the profession to change, but at the same time it is hard to believe it can *actually* change. That is probably because our mind has unconsciously identified a hundred cons, pitfalls, and things that would make such change *implausible*—or at minimum, really difficult (e.g., to be honest, I'm already worrying about the billing system! How do we fix that puzzle? Is it even possible?). But we don't have to aim for perfection because perfection doesn't exist. We just need to start somewhere. That's where progress truly lies. And I get it, the statement of "*let's face it, things are as they are*" has been ingrained in us for so long. But are things as they are; or, are they also what we make of them?

If we wait for the perfect solution, we'll simply end up procrastinating.[162] While the rates of anxiety, depression, and suicide in the legal profession are still there, we can start by understanding how our (legal) brains are wired, or what our repetitive thought patterns are. We can start by being honest about our anxiety and depression. We can start to open up about it because as social beings, we heal in

162 Raise your hand if you've been involved in the toxic relationship between *Perfectionism & Procrastination* (I'm raising mine, obvi…Lol).

community. We can look at our minds, face-to-face, and say *"Hey baby, please stop with the negative hypothetical scenarios! They have not even happened! We're here now, and it's all good! I love you"*—or similar. We can start by telling ourselves that we're doing our best; and that things can get better. We can improve ourselves, from the inside. We can start right there.

And no, things will not be perfect, but trying is good enough. Making progress is *brilliant*—and enough. Some might have really hard situations at work, abusive bosses, or an insane caseload; but regardless of those, you can still build inner resilience and a more supportive mindset towards yourself. You can ask for support. You can proclaim that things can—and will—get better for you. And while we've all developed our own unique ways of coping with stress, I invite you to consider if those ways are serving you in your daily life and in the long term. How do you process anxious thoughts or challenging feelings? Are your boundaries clear and consistent? Do you know what aspects of your life drain your soul? What is your inner dialogue when things get rough?

Here's the thing: sometimes being stuck in a repetitive ball of pain is worse than the fear of taking a leap into uncertainty. I know that's a pretty abstract statement, but what I mean is that you don't need to accept the fallacy that *lawyers are inevitably stressed-out and unhappy*. You can rise from that. You can—and deserve—to be happy and free. I mean, why else do you think you came to this Earth? Improving oneself is not an easy road, but as one of my favorite legal writing professors once told me, '*if it doesn't feel challenging, it's because there's not much growth in it.*' And if want to journey with me and improve the way you talk to yourself through emotional intelligence, I'd love to hear from you (espy@esperanzaishope.com).

For current & future law students:

For starters, let me remind you that neither the Law School Administration Council ("LSAC"), law schools, or any other institution do not—and will never—determine your worth, your resilience or power. Now, here are a couple of reminders that have served me and my friends well:

If you are feeling inferior or navigating the *comparisonitis mindf*ck*, please know this:

The fact that you're surrounded by bright and hard-working individuals does *not* undermine your intelligence. Rather, it's an indication that you're exactly where you need to be: surrounded by bright minds, like your very own. Comparison is a form of self-sabotage; and the uniqueness behind your experience, path, and human essence is—and will always be—sacred. Can you take a minute and think of one thing about yourself you're truly proud of? Please say it to yourself.

If you're feeling like you want to quit, please know this:

Your biggest asset is your *grit*. Grit is the cognitive ability that has made you pursue your lawyer dream in the first place. It's the perseverance you have exercised towards that goal, despite the obstacles, distractions, and difficulties.

When alive, my dad once said to me: "*You are not a failure if you keep fighting.*" Thus, although this law school journey might get lonely and difficult, you are not a failure if you keep fighting for your lawyer dream. And always remember: you are not alone. Please keep going.

Wherever you are in your law school journey, I am rooting for you. You can find resources and our online courses on how to succeed in law school at www.esperanzaishope.com. If you have any questions, please feel free to reach us on our IG inbox or directly at espy@esperanzaishope.com. I hope to see you in our IG community [@esperanza.ishope] or on the zoom screen soon *-^

For law schools and those who care about law students:

My hope is that, as new and more conscious generations start demanding better care from their law schools, each institution will be compelled to create its own curated curriculums to attract prospective law students (who are also their paying customers). My hope is that law school's emphasis on mental health and emotional skills will become another factor incoming law students will consider when choosing to pay significant amounts of law school tuition. As law students gain more bargaining power, they will be able to differentiate between performative and genuine institutional support; and thereby make a well-informed decision about their chosen institution's commitment to their mental health and emotional growth as future attorneys.

I know we can't completely change a flawed system in a day, in a year, or maybe in a decade. But we can start by teaching students basic, emotional intelligence skills that will help them offset the negative impact of legal education. For example, those teachings could include tools such as:

- Self-awareness to identify detrimental thoughts, vicious cycles and perfectionistic or self-loathing narratives;

- Self-management to reframe those narratives and convert them into more compassionate and empowering inner dialogues; as well as to introduce techniques to calm the nervous system when we're experiencing high levels of anxiety in any given moment;

- Resilience to enforce growth mindsets that will allow us to surpass the obstacles that the legal profession will inevitably bring and integrate the fact that as humans, we are not perfect, nor are we machines who can work 24/7 without taking a break; and/or

- Empathy to create more supportive and authentic environments for both our colleagues and our clients.

We can do that. We can start right there, at the very root. We can start at the very beginning of any lawyer's journey: *law school.* So why don't we?

As hopefully expressed throughout this book, I am very passionate about supporting students. Thus, if you are part of a law school or an institution who would like to offer emotional intelligence tools to students and their future practice, I'd love to help. Please contact me at espy@esperanzaishope.com for courses, or any collaborations, speaking or writing engagements on topics related to law and emotional intelligence!

For all of you who have read these pages:

Thank you for investing your time with me and this work.[163]
It means a lot.

Wishing you light and strength for the journey,
Esperanza (Espy)

163 If you feel like sharing your experience or thoughts on this book with me, please contact me at the email above. I know this might sound like the typical, superficially nice thing to say; but I mean it!

Reminder: if you use any of the teachings, exercises, or material contained in this book, please kindly cite or credit this work. Thank you for respecting the effort and time invested in creating this resource :-).

I know I already said goodbye, but I wanted to share one last thing with you:

It is in our wounds and vulnerability where our true power lies. That's where this book came from.

May you find freedom, inner peace and unconditional self-love wherever you go.

Abrazo,
E

Made in the USA
Coppell, TX
16 July 2024

34727852R00152